# RICHMOND
# FCE

## PRACTICE TESTS

Teacher's Book

**Diana L Fried-Booth**

# Contents

# Introduction

The *Richmond FCE Practice Tests* Student's Book contains five practice tests for the Cambridge First Certificate in English examination. The tests reflect the kind of materials and tasks that students can expect to come across when they take the FCE exam itself and are designed to help your students prepare for the exam by familiarising them with the type of tasks they will have to complete, as well as the amount of time allowed for each paper.

This Teacher's Book contains everything you need to help your students get the most from the *Richmond FCE Practice Tests*. The following pages contain a detailed, photocopiable introduction to the FCE exam, including helpful advice for students on how to tackle each part of each paper.

In addition, full-colour visual material, listening transcripts and answer keys are provided for all five tests, as well as mark schemes for the Writing and Speaking Papers (pages 62–63). To help familiarise students with the format of the exam paper, a photocopiable answer sheet for Writing Part 2 is provided on page 11, while sample Cambridge ESOL exam answer sheets for the Reading, Use of English and Listening Papers are reproduced on pages 12–16.

## Exam structure

Each test contains the five papers which comprise the complete FCE examination: Reading, Writing, Use of English, Listening and Speaking. You are advised to set Papers 1, 2 and 3 in the order in which students will take them in the exam itself. Papers 4 and 5 need not be done on the same day.

Each paper is worth 40 marks, and the marks for the individual papers are added together to form a total mark out of 200. The raw scores for each paper are scaled so that each paper receives equal weighting.

## Results

There are three pass grades: A, B, C; and three fail grades: D, E, and U. A minimum grade C pass corresponds to approximately 60% of the total mark.

When students get their results, they will be notified if they have done particularly well or badly on individual papers.

Students can take either a paper-based or computer-based examination.

## EACH PAPER COMPRISES THE FOLLOWING SECTIONS:

### PAPER 1

| | |
|---|---|
| **Reading** | **Content** |
| | 30 questions based on 3 long texts. The paper is approximately 2,000 words long. |
| **Time** | 1 hour |

**Task**

**PART 1** 8  4-option multiple choice questions on a text

**PART 2** 7 questions reordering sentences which have been removed from a text

**PART 3** 15 questions which require selecting items from a list and matching them to sections of text(s)

### PAPER 2

| | |
|---|---|
| **Writing** | **Content** |
| | 2 writing tasks: 1 compulsory and 1 from a choice of 5 different tasks which include a question based on set texts |
| **Time** | 1 hour 20 minutes |

**Task**

**PART 1** Writing a letter or an email based on written information which may occasionally include illustrations or other visual material (120-150 words)

**PART 2** A choice of questions based on: an article, an email, an essay, a letter, a report, a review, a story. (120-180 words)

# PAPER 3

| Use of English | **Content** |
|---|---|
| | 42 questions based on 4 separate parts |
| **Time** | 45 minutes |

**Task**

**PART 1** 12 questions based on a text containing 12 gaps with 4-option multiple choice items for each gap

**PART 2** 12 questions based on a text with 12 missing words to be supplied

**PART 3** 10 word building questions based on filling in missing words in a text, using the root of the word which is printed in the margin beside each gap

**PART 4** 8 questions based on completing a sentence using a key word (which is supplied) so that the rewritten sentence means the same as the original one

# PAPER 4

| Listening | **Content** |
|---|---|
| | 30 questions based on 4 recorded texts drawn from a variety of sources: talks, advertisements, interviews, phone messages, lectures, speeches, announcements, news broadcasts, conversations, etc. |
| **Time** | Approximately 40 minutes |

**Task**

**PART 1** 8 3-option multiple choice questions based on 8 short recordings with 1 or 2 speakers

**PART 2** 10 gap-fill questions based on a recording with 1 or 2 speakers

**PART 3** 5 multiple match questions based on listening to 5 short recordings and selecting the correct answer from a list of 6 options

**PART 4** 7 3-option multiple choice questions based on a recording with 1 or more speakers

# PAPER 5

| Speaking | **Content** |
|---|---|
| | 4 parts taken in pairs with 2 examiners present, one who conducts the interview and one who assesses |
| **Time** | 14 minutes |

**Task**

**PART 1** Giving personal information and talking about oneself

**PART 2** Expressing opinions and attitudes in response to a pair of colour photos and taking turns to talk for up to a minute each

**PART 3** Talking to each other in response to a visual stimulus, e.g. diagram, drawing, etc.

**PART 4** Talking to the interviewer based on the discussion arising out of Part 3

# Organisation

The following pages contain detailed information about what to expect in the FCE exam, as well as helpful advice on how to complete each part of each paper. Until you become completely familiar with the content of each paper, you should always remind yourself about the various tasks before you begin a practice paper.

# Exam advice

## PAPER 1  Reading

### PART 1

Read the instructions carefully as they will tell you what the passage is going to be about.

Read the passage through carefully **without** looking at the questions.

Don't spend a long time worrying about words which you don't know. It may be that you will be able to answer the questions without knowing a few of the words anyway.

Look at the questions. Each question has 4 possible answers and you have to choose the one correct alternative and mark A, B, C or D on your answer sheet.

When you first look at a question, you may have an idea of the answer from what you have read. Don't be tempted to guess, but go back to the passage and focus in detail on the part of the text which contains the information to answer the question.

If the question is testing your understanding of the whole passage, skim through the passage and don't just focus on the beginning or the ending of the text.

If there is a question such as 'What does 'it' in line 22 refer to?', read the few sentences surrounding the word *it* particularly carefully, so that you follow the line of argument before choosing the answer.

The 'wrong' options will be written in such a way that they could almost seem right and they will also use the information which is contained in the passage.

If you are unsure of a correct option for one question, then try to work out why the other answers could be wrong; there will only be one correct answer.

If you try and fill in two answers on your answer sheet, you will get no marks at all for that question – even if one of the answers is the correct one!

### PART 2

Read through the text slowly and carefully and try to focus on the main idea in each paragraph.

Look at the list of what has been removed and remember that one of the sentences / paragraphs in the list will be extra and therefore remain unused.

Reread the text a paragraph at a time and look carefully at the grammatical structures which come **before** and **after the gaps**. There may be words or phrases which will help you to identify the missing information, or references to a sequence of events, places or people. The sentence links should also help you to decide what has been removed.

If you have time, read back the paragraph to yourself (silently!), putting in the missing information as you go to check that what you are reading makes sense.

### PART 3

Don't be put off by the volume of material in this part of the paper.

You are not expected to know all the vocabulary in the text(s).

Learn to scan through the material which is redundant (not relevant), until you come to the specific information which you do need to answer the questions.

The questions come before the text(s) and will not be in the same order as the information in the texts, so be prepared to scan the text(s) a number of times before you find the specific information you need.

As the same information can be used more than once, the amount of information remains the same throughout the task.

## PAPER 2  Writing

The two parts of this paper carry equal marks and you have to write your answers on the ruled sheets which are included with your question paper.

For Part 2, do not forget to write the number of the question you have chosen to answer in the box at the top of the page.

An examiner will assess what you write with reference to two different mark schemes. The General Impression Mark Scheme, which focuses on the overall level of your writing, is used in conjunction with another mark scheme, the Task Specific Mark Scheme which focuses on the criteria relevant to a particular question.

You can expect the Task Specific Mark Scheme to focus on the content relevant to that task, appropriate vocabulary, range of grammatical structure, spelling and punctuation, appropriate style, coherent organisation of material, the effect on the reader, appropriate length and presentation.

### PART 1  *Compulsory question*

In this question you will have to write a letter or an email in response to a situation which is described for you in the form of additional information like advertisements, notices, letters, notes, emails or even pictures or drawings.

The style in which you have to write this letter or email will be fairly formal. The task requires you to write a letter in order to achieve something, so make sure you read the instructions carefully. You may be asked to write a letter making a complaint, asking for information, giving information, describing or explaining a situation, and so on.

Read all the information so that you can clearly identify the situation, the task and who you are writing to.

All the information that you need in order to answer the question is supplied for you; you don't need to write any dates or addresses.

Don't be tempted to copy out large sections from the information printed on your question paper: it is there to give you a clear framework for your own writing.

Make sure you cover all the points which will need to be included to complete the task as fully as possible.

Keep within the number of words (120-150) which you are asked to write. By the time you take the FCE you should have an idea of what this number of words looks like in your handwriting, so you don't waste time in the exam counting the number of words you have written. If you write too much, a line will be drawn across your page at the point where the length is correct and the examiner will assess your answer above that line.

### PART 2

In this part of the paper you have a choice of question; don't choose a set book question unless you have prepared for it.

Choose a question which genuinely interests you or which you feel you know something about.

Look carefully at the kind of reader you are asked to write for and the reason for writing.

Underline or colour in the key words in the question.

The kind of writing task, i.e. report, article, informal letter, short story, essay, etc. is stated for you: make sure you are absolutely clear about what you are writing and who you are writing it for.

If you have time, make a brief plan and check that you intend to include material that is relevant to the question.

Try to demonstrate your range of grammatical structures and vocabulary and show the examiner how much you know.

## PAPER 3    Use of English

The passages in this paper are usually taken from authentic sources like newspaper articles and magazines and will reflect different kinds of writing such as letters, articles, advertisements, reports, etc.

There are 42 questions altogether.

### PART 1    Multiple choice cloze

The title of the passage will give you an idea of what you are going to read about. Read through the complete passage (approximately 200 words) fairly quickly in order to understand the context, and look at the example which will have been completed for you.

The task requires you to choose the missing word from a choice of 4 words for each of the 12 gaps. The focus of the exercise is on vocabulary (nouns, adjectives, a collocation or fixed phrase, etc.), although there will also be a few questions which test your knowledge of the grammatical structure of the sentence.

You may recognise what some of the missing words are likely to be before you look at the multiple choice items.

Concentrate on answering the questions which you are fairly sure of before you spend time on those which you find more difficult.

Don't just concentrate on looking at what is written immediately before a gap; it is equally important to look at what comes immediately after a gap.

If there are words which you don't know, try 'hearing' the various alternatives in your head. Although it's not a reliable technique for answering examination questions, sometimes your feel for the language may help you eliminate the wrong answers.

Don't leave any questions unanswered; **always** attempt a question – in this part of the paper there's a 25% chance of guessing the right answer!

### PART 2    Open cloze

This question requires you to read a passage (approximately 200 words) and fill in the missing words in the 12 gaps. The focus of this exercise is on your knowledge of grammatical structure.

Look at the title. What is the passage going to be about? If you don't recognise the word(s) in the title, don't panic but look at the opening few lines of the passage for the answer.

Without trying to fill in any of the words, read through the complete passage quite quickly to get an idea of the content. Pay particular attention to the structure of what you are reading and how the sentences are linked together to develop the writer's argument.

The answer will always be **one** word. You won't lose marks for putting the wrong answer, but you will lose marks if you write two words on the answer sheet even if they both seem correct.

On a second, slower reading, fill in the missing words which you are confident of by writing them in the appropriate numbered spaces on your separate answer sheet.

The chances are you will find some gaps easier than others. Be a language detective and use all the clues available: do you need a noun, an adverb, a preposition, a linking word, part of a phrasal verb, etc. to complete the sentence? If it is a verb, which tense is it likely to be in? If you can identify the kind of word (and even if you can't), then make a sensible guess.

Finally, when you have filled in all the missing words, read the passage through again. Does it make sense and read correctly? And remember to check that you have **spelt each word correctly**.

## PART 3    *Word formation*

In this part of the paper, your vocabulary is tested by your ability to form words to fill gaps in a text. The base form of the word is printed (in capitals) beside the line in which the word is missing.

The passage will have a title, so first of all look at this and then read the passage through once very carefully to make sure you understand the content.

The word which you have to build must fit the grammar of the sentence, so look at the structure either side of the gap for clues as to whether you need to form a noun from a verb base, an adverb from a noun, an adjective from a verb base, etc.

If you don't immediately recognise a word, use what you know about word building. For example, most adverbs will need *-ly* added, but if the printed base word ends in *-y* (e.g. *beauty*), you will also need to make spelling changes (e.g. beauti*fully*).

Make sure you know the common ways in which the English language forms nouns, e.g. using *-ment*, *-ence*, *-tion*, etc.

Does the word need a prefix like *un-* or *im-* if the meaning is negative? Or maybe it needs a suffix like *-less* to make the meaning negative.

Check whether the word needs to be singular or plural if you are required to fill the gap with a noun.

When you have decided what the word is, write it on your separate answer sheet, making sure that you transfer the correct word into its numbered space and that you have **spelt it correctly**.

## PART 4    *Key word transformations*

In this part there are 8 questions which test your ability to deal with vocabulary and grammatical structure.

You are asked to transform sentences by changing one grammatical structure to another using a **key word**. The key word is printed in **bold type** below the first sentence, and the rewritten sentence is incomplete. Using this key word, you have to fill in the gap in the incomplete sentence, so that the new sentence has a similar meaning to the original one.

You must **not make any changes to the key word**.

You must use between 2 and 5 words (including the key word) to complete the sentence and you need to transfer only these words onto your answer sheet. The beginning and the end of the new sentence will be printed on your question paper.

If you use a contraction, for example *he's*, this counts as 2 words.

Make sure the new sentence includes **all** the points from the original sentence and check that you have **spelt the missing words correctly**.

## PAPER 4    Listening

The Listening paper consists of 4 parts. You will listen to a recording which lasts about 40 minutes, including the 5 minutes at the end of the test for you to transfer your answers to the separate answer sheet. You hear everything twice and the instructions are both spoken on the recording and printed on your question paper.

There are 30 questions altogether.

## PART 1

This part consists of 8 short extracts and 8 3-option multiple choice questions. The questions are designed to test your ability to identify various things such as the situation, who is speaking, the reason for what the speaker is saying, whether an opinion or a feeling is being expressed, or where the conversation is taking place.

Before the recording begins, you will be allowed time to read through the questions. It's really important that you use this time to prepare yourself for what you are going to hear, and at the same time try to identify the situation or the context for what you will hear.

Focus on one question at a time. The fact that each short extract is different means that if you fail to understand one of the situations, there is plenty of opportunity to have another go and get all the others right. So don't panic and allow one 'problem' to affect everything else.

The extracts are short – about half a minute each – and may be either one speaker (monologue) or two speakers (dialogue). Each extract is repeated in turn and you are told the number of each question as the recording proceeds, so you can't get lost!

On the first listening try to pick out the correct option, and use the second listening to check your answer.

## PART 2

In this part you will hear either a single speaker or a conversation between 2 or 4 speakers which lasts for about 3 minutes. The task consists of writing short answers to 10 questions. These questions are based on completing sentences.

Use the preparation time to look carefully at the kind of information you are going to need in order to fill in the gaps. What kind of words can you expect to write? Will you have to listen for how old someone is, for the place where two people are going to meet, for the title of a course that someone is going to do, etc?

By reading the questions, can you guess what the piece is likely to be about?

If you look at the length of the spaces where you have to write your answers on the answer sheet (see page 118), you will see that you are not expected to write more than one or two words at the most.

You may lose marks for words that are incorrectly spelt.

## PART 3

This part of the paper consists of 5 short extracts (about half a minute each), either monologues or short dialogues, and a multiple matching task. There are 5 questions and a list of 6 possible answers to choose from. You hear the complete recording of all 5 extracts twice.

Use the preparation time to read through the list of answers so that you have an idea of what you will be specifically listening for in order to match the extract with the appropriate answer.

Read (and listen to) the instructions carefully as that will identify the context for the extracts.

As you listen for the first time, try to select the correct answer, and as you listen for the second time, check your understanding by focusing on the information in the listening text which corresponds with the information in the answer.

The answers are lettered A-F, and one answer will not be needed; don't use one answer more than once.

## PART 4

The last part of the Listening paper consists of either a monologue or a conversation involving 2 or 3 speakers and lasts about 3 minutes. It will have 7 3-option multiple choice questions. The questions will always be objective and you will not have to write any words or short answers.

Use the preparation time to read through the questions. In this part of the test you can expect the questions to focus on your ability to understand both the gist and the main ideas contained in the whole piece, as well as the attitudes, feelings and opinions expressed by the speaker(s).

There will be fewer questions which test your understanding of detail and specific information, so listen very carefully for the attitudes and moods of each speaker not only through what they say, but also through the intonation which they use to express their feelings.

The questions will follow the order in which you hear the information.

## PAPER 5   Speaking

The Speaking paper is taken with a partner and lasts approximately 14 minutes. It is divided into 4 parts and there are 2 examiners present; one examiner acts as the interlocutor and the other examiner, who does not take part in the conversation, carries out the assessment. Whether or not you know your partner in the interview makes no difference to your assessment as you are assessed independently.

### PART 1   3 minutes

In this part you and your partner will be asked to talk about yourself, your interests and your personal and family background. The examiner will speak to each of you in turn.

### PART 2   4 minutes

In this part you and your partner will each be given 2 photographs in turn.

Look carefully at your photos, listen to what the examiner asks you to talk about in relation to the photographs and look at the question printed above the photographs. You have to talk for about a minute each.

If you are not sure what you have been asked to do, then ask for the instruction to be repeated. You do not lose marks by asking for something to be repeated, but if you sit in silence for too long, the assessor will not be able to judge whether you actually have the language skills to talk about the photographs.

Don't expect to just describe what you can see in the photos; you will also be asked to express opinions about the situations, and the similarities and/or contrasts between the photographs. At the end of each long turn you are asked a short question about your partner's photograph and you should respond appropriately – sometimes the question requires no more than a simple *Yes* or *No*.

### PART 3   3 minutes

In Part 3 the interlocutor will give you some new material to look at. It may be another photograph or a group of photographs, a drawing or drawings, an advertisement, a leaflet, etc. The instructions for the task are printed at the top of the sheet.

You and your partner are expected to work together on whatever task you are given; the interlocutor will listen but not join in.

You need to show that you can take turns in discussing things with your partner, that you can agree or disagree if necessary and that you can express opinions and exchange information together.

You might be asked to plan something, to solve a particular problem or to prioritise, that is to place things – like holiday destinations, for example – in order of importance from your own point of view.

Don't try to include the interlocutor in what you are saying, but you will be asked to speak so that both the interlocutor and assessor can hear you.

Be supportive towards your partner by trying to use language which shows that you understand that you are working together, for example: *What do you think? What about you? I'm not sure I agree with you. Shall we take this point/picture first? So what's our conclusion? Yes, that's what I think, too. So, what shall we decide?*

Don't dominate the conversation.

Don't feel too shy to say what you really think.

Don't worry if the examiner interrupts you, as you only have about 3 minutes for this part; on the other hand, don't rush into making conclusions too early in the conversation.

**PART 4** *4 minutes*

In the final part the interlocutor will join in the discussion and extend and develop the theme or the topic which you have been talking about in the third part. The skills which you have to use in Part 4 are very similar to those you used in Part 3, but this time it is a three-way discussion.

Listen to what the others have to say and try to reply appropriately and naturally. You may be asked to expand on something which you previously mentioned or to consider another viewpoint.

At the end of the test the examiners will say thank you and say goodbye. Don't ask for or expect any comment on how you have performed.

## Assessment

You will be assessed on the following criteria across the complete Speaking Test:

**Grammar and vocabulary:** You need to show the examiners that you can use the grammatical structures and vocabulary appropriate to this level with sufficient accuracy in order to carry out the tasks.

**Discourse management:** You need to show the examiners that you can organise what you want to say. Your sentences may be short or long (depending on what is appropriate) but they must be coherently linked.

**Pronunciation:** You need to show that you can produce individual sounds and use appropriate stress, rhythm and intonation to convey what you mean, despite the influence of your mother tongue.

**Interactive communication:** You need to show that you are able to interact with other people, that you know how to take turns in a conversation and that you can respond to questions, negotiate with a partner and initiate ideas.

The assessor awards a mark for each criterion (i.e. 4 marks) and the interlocutor awards just one impression mark. The mark represents 20% of the total mark for the FCE.

## Computerised answer sheets

In both the Student's Book and the Teacher's Book, there are examples of the computerised mark sheets which you will have to use in the examination for the Reading, Use of English and Listening papers. Make sure that you know how to fill in a computerised mark sheet using a soft pencil.

The small boxes which you have to fill in are called lozenges. If you make a mistake, rub it out with a clean rubber; don't use white-out fluid.

In Paper 1, the Reading paper, if you decide to copy your answers from your question paper onto your answer sheet (instead of answering directly onto your answer sheet), make sure that you copy across very carefully and that your answers don't get out of order.

In Papers 3 and 4, Use of English and Listening, don't write outside the spaces which are allowed for your answers and remember to write clearly. If your handwriting is very big or occasionally difficult to read, you must be prepared to modify it in your own interests.

In Paper 4, Listening, you are allowed five minutes at the end to transfer your answers, so don't try to fill in the answer sheet while you are listening to the recordings.

*For further information about the FCE, write to:*

*University of Cambridge*
*ESOL Examinations*
*1 Hills Road*
*Cambridge*
*CB1 2EU*
*UK*
*www.CambridgeESOL.org*

| Question | |
|---|---|

**UNIVERSITY** *of* **CAMBRIDGE**
ESOL Examinations

**Do not write in this box**

SAMPLE

**Candidate Name**
If not already printed, write name
in CAPITALS and complete the
Candidate No. grid (in pencil).

**Candidate Signature**

**Examination Title**

**Centre**

Supervisor:

If the candidate is ABSENT or has WITHDRAWN shade here

**Centre No.**

**Candidate No.**

**Examination Details**

| 0 | 0 | 0 | 0 |
| 1 | 1 | 1 | 1 |
| 2 | 2 | 2 | 2 |
| 3 | 3 | 3 | 3 |
| 4 | 4 | 4 | 4 |
| 5 | 5 | 5 | 5 |
| 6 | 6 | 6 | 6 |
| 7 | 7 | 7 | 7 |
| 8 | 8 | 8 | 8 |
| 9 | 9 | 9 | 9 |

## Candidate Answer Sheet

### Instructions

**Use a PENCIL (B or HB).**

Mark ONE letter for each question.

For example, if you think B is the right answer to the question, mark your answer sheet like this:

0   A B C D E F G H

Rub out any answer you wish to change using an eraser.

| 1 | A B C D E F G H |
| 2 | A B C D E F G H |
| 3 | A B C D E F G H |
| 4 | A B C D E F G H |
| 5 | A B C D E F G H |
| 6 | A B C D E F G H |
| 7 | A B C D E F G H |
| 8 | A B C D E F G H |
| 9 | A B C D E F G H |
| 10 | A B C D E F G H |
| 11 | A B C D E F G H |
| 12 | A B C D E F G H |
| 13 | A B C D E F G H |
| 14 | A B C D E F G H |
| 15 | A B C D E F G H |
| 16 | A B C D E F G H |
| 17 | A B C D E F G H |
| 18 | A B C D E F G H |
| 19 | A B C D E F G H |
| 20 | A B C D E F G H |

| 21 | A B C D E F G H |
| 22 | A B C D E F G H |
| 23 | A B C D E F G H |
| 24 | A B C D E F G H |
| 25 | A B C D E F G H |
| 26 | A B C D E F G H |
| 27 | A B C D E F G H |
| 28 | A B C D E F G H |
| 29 | A B C D E F G H |
| 30 | A B C D E F G H |
| 31 | A B C D E F G H |
| 32 | A B C D E F G H |
| 33 | A B C D E F G H |
| 34 | A B C D E F G H |
| 35 | A B C D E F G H |
| 36 | A B C D E F G H |
| 37 | A B C D E F G H |
| 38 | A B C D E F G H |
| 39 | A B C D E F G H |
| 40 | A B C D E F G H |

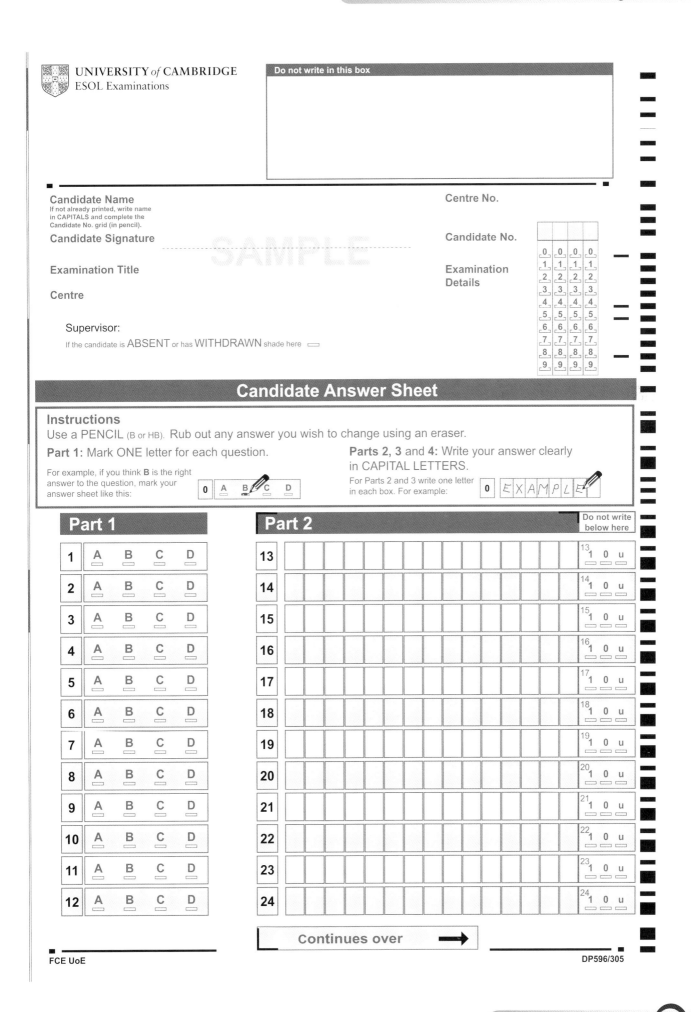

## Part 3

| | | Do not write below here |
|---|---|---|
| 25 | | 25 1 0 u |
| 26 | | 26 1 0 u |
| 27 | | 27 1 0 u |
| 28 | | 28 1 0 u |
| 29 | | 29 1 0 u |
| 30 | | 30 1 0 u |
| 31 | | 31 1 0 u |
| 32 | | 32 1 0 u |
| 33 | | 33 1 0 u |
| 34 | | 34 1 0 u |

## Part 4

SAMPLE

| | | Do not write below here |
|---|---|---|
| 35 | | 35 2 1 0 u |
| 36 | | 36 2 1 0 u |
| 37 | | 37 2 1 0 u |
| 38 | | 38 2 1 0 u |
| 39 | | 39 2 1 0 u |
| 40 | | 40 2 1 0 u |
| 41 | | 41 2 1 0 u |
| 42 | | 42 2 1 0 u |

denote Print Limited 0121 520 5100

14

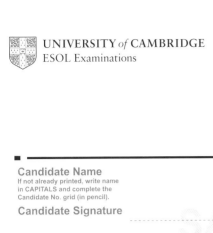

UNIVERSITY *of* CAMBRIDGE
ESOL Examinations

**Candidate Name**
If not already printed, write name
in CAPITALS and complete the
Candidate No. grid (in pencil).

**Candidate Signature**

SAMPLE

**Examination Title**

**Centre**

Supervisor:

If the candidate is ABSENT or has WITHDRAWN shade here ▭

**Centre No.**

**Candidate No.**

**Examination Details**

| | | | |
|---|---|---|---|
| 0 | 0 | 0 | 0 |
| 1 | 1 | 1 | 1 |
| 2 | 2 | 2 | 2 |
| 3 | 3 | 3 | 3 |
| 4 | 4 | 4 | 4 |
| 5 | 5 | 5 | 5 |
| 6 | 6 | 6 | 6 |
| 7 | 7 | 7 | 7 |
| 8 | 8 | 8 | 8 |
| 9 | 9 | 9 | 9 |

Test version: A B C D E F J K L M N     Special arrangements: S H

## Candidate Answer Sheet

---

### Instructions

Use a PENCIL (B or HB).
Rub out any answer you wish to change using an eraser.

**Parts 1, 3** and **4:**
Mark ONE letter for each question.

For example, if you think **B** is the
right answer to the question, mark
your answer sheet like this:

| 0 | A | B | C |
|---|---|---|---|

**Part 2:**
Write your answer clearly in CAPITAL LETTERS.

Write one letter or number in each box.
If the answer has more than one word, leave one
box empty between words.

For example:

| 0 | N | U | M | B | E | R | | 1 | 2 | | | |
|---|---|---|---|---|---|---|---|---|---|---|---|---|

**Turn this sheet over to start.**

## Part 1

| | A | B | C |
|---|---|---|---|
| 1 | A | B | C |
| 2 | A | B | C |
| 3 | A | B | C |
| 4 | A | B | C |
| 5 | A | B | C |
| 6 | A | B | C |
| 7 | A | B | C |
| 8 | A | B | C |

## Part 2 (Remember to write in CAPITAL LETTERS or numbers)

Do not write below here

| 9 | | 9 1 0 u |
| 10 | | 10 1 0 u |
| 11 | | 11 1 0 u |
| 12 | | 12 1 0 u |
| 13 | | 13 1 0 u |
| 14 | | 14 1 0 u |
| 15 | | 15 1 0 u |
| 16 | | 16 1 0 u |
| 17 | | 17 1 0 u |
| 18 | | 18 1 0 u |

## Part 3

| | A | B | C | D | E | F |
|---|---|---|---|---|---|---|
| 19 | A | B | C | D | E | F |
| 20 | A | B | C | D | E | F |
| 21 | A | B | C | D | E | F |
| 22 | A | B | C | D | E | F |
| 23 | A | B | C | D | E | F |

## Part 4

| | A | B | C |
|---|---|---|---|
| 24 | A | B | C |
| 25 | A | B | C |
| 26 | A | B | C |
| 27 | A | B | C |
| 28 | A | B | C |
| 29 | A | B | C |
| 30 | A | B | C |

denote Print Limited 0121 520 5100

**The following pages contain the material for the Speaking test.**

Why is each kind of entertainment popular with different groups of people?

1

2

Why do people sometimes choose to be alone?

3

4

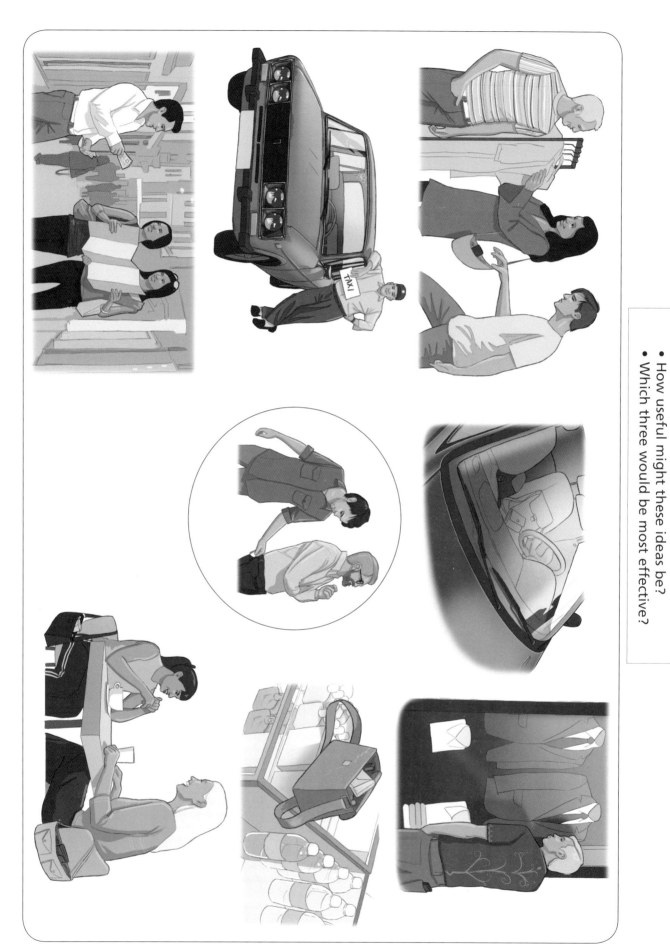

- How useful might these ideas be?
- Which three would be most effective?

What kind of lives do these young people lead?

1

2

What are the different people doing?

3

4

- How helpful might these suggestions be?
- Which two would you choose to spend the money on?

How are these people choosing to spend their free time?

1

2

Why are these people dressed like this?

3

4

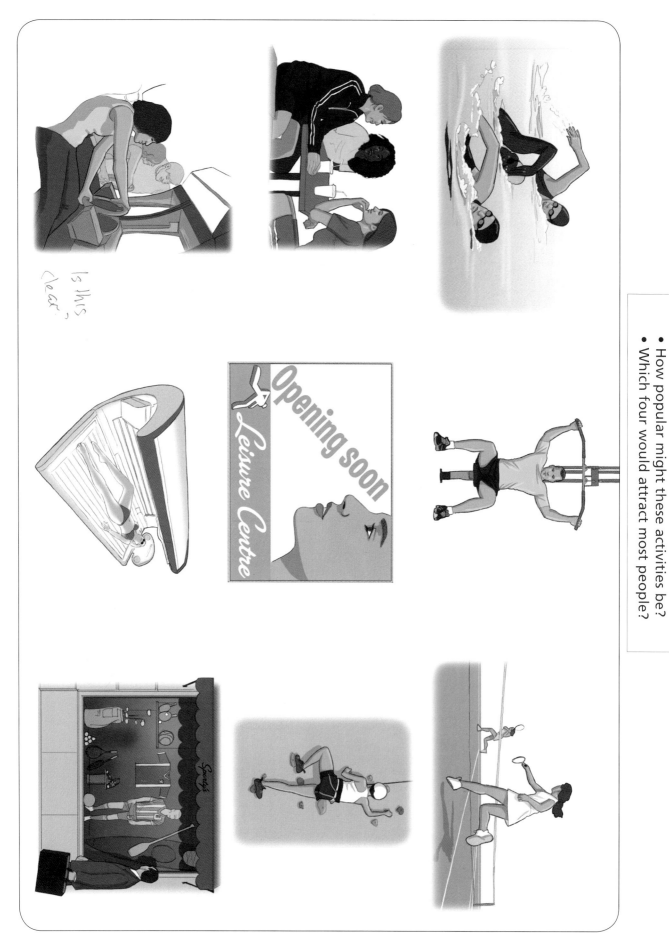

- How popular might these activities be?
- Which four would attract most people?

Why do parents and children enjoy doing things together?

1

2

looks like grandparents

Why do people like shopping in markets?

better
to have
people
like
cards?

3

4

cover
brand name

- How successful might these pictures be?
- Which three would be most suitable?

too young for FCE

5

Why have the people chosen to enjoy themselves in this way?

1

2

What are the advantages and disadvantages of living in the country?

3

4

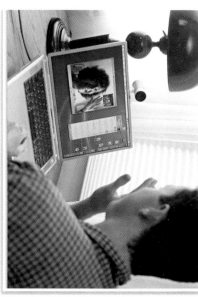

- What are the different ways people can communicate with each other?
- Which three ways are most suitable for young people?

# Transcripts

## PRACTICE TEST 1

This is the Richmond First Certificate Practice Test One. Listening. I'm going to give you the instructions for this test. I'll introduce each part of the test and give you time to look at the questions. At the start of each piece you'll hear this sound:

*Sound effect*

You'll hear each piece twice.

Remember, while you're listening, write your answers on the question paper. You'll have 5 minutes at the end of the test to copy your answers onto the separate answer sheet.

There will now be a pause. Please ask any questions now, because you must not speak during the test.

PAUSE 5 SECONDS

Now open your question paper and look at Part 1.

### PART 1

You'll hear people talking in eight different situations. For questions 1-8, choose the best answer, A, B or C.

1 You hear a woman talking to a supermarket manager. What is she complaining about?
   A  soft pears and lemons
   B  rotten oranges and apples
   C  brown lemons and grapes

PAUSE 5 SECONDS

I'm afraid I've lost my receipt but last week I bought a lot of fruit – pears, oranges, apples and so on – and within a few days some of the fruit was completely rotten. Not all of it, admittedly, but the grapes and surprisingly the lemons went brown and I had to throw them out. Well, actually I've brought the oranges back and as you'll see they've gone very soft and brown as well. So I was wondering about a refund.

PAUSE 2 SECONDS – REPEAT Q.1 – PAUSE 2 SECONDS

2 You hear a man cancelling a hotel booking. What is the reason for the cancellation?
   A  His wife has to go into hospital.
   B  His wife has to go away suddenly.
   C  His wife has been in an accident.

PAUSE 5 SECONDS

... and, yes, I'm afraid I shall have to cancel the reservation. ... No, I know I shall lose the deposit, but my wife has to go abroad rather unexpectedly. One of her friends has been hurt in a climbing accident and is in hospital, so quite naturally my wife is flying out to visit her ...

PAUSE 2 SECONDS – REPEAT Q.2 – PAUSE 2 SECONDS

3 You are visiting an art exhibition. What does your friend say about it?
   A  It's expensive.
   B  It's too modern.
   C  It's meaningless.

PAUSE 5 SECONDS

Oh, let's go and have a coffee. This is a complete waste of time and money. I'm fed up with wandering through these huge rooms – and for what? In the first room there was that pile of bricks, and nothing else, and then there were those old bicycle tyres – and now there's this heap of newspapers. And what's more, there's no information on any of it.

PAUSE 2 SECONDS – REPEAT Q.3 – PAUSE 2 SECONDS

4 You overhear two people talking. What are they discussing?
   A  a car
   B  a bike
   C  a fridge

PAUSE 5 SECONDS

**Man:** It's one of the latest models and is proving very popular.

**Woman:** I'm not terribly keen on the colour.

**Man:** Well, they do others in the range, although the metallic colours are more expensive.

**Woman:** Perhaps I could try it out. Get a feel for how it performs.

**Man:** By all means. You take a seat behind the wheel and I'll get one of my colleagues to join you.

PAUSE 2 SECONDS – REPEAT Q.4 – PAUSE 2 SECONDS

5 You hear a teacher talking to some students. What is he telling them to do?
   A  write down some information
   B  look at a new film
   C  copy out some information

PAUSE 5 SECONDS

Right, now last week we looked at that film on the rainforest and this week I want to begin by going over some of the key points which you wrote down. Then, if you turn to page 17, you'll see the map which has all the world's rainforests on it. That needs to be copied into your notebooks and labelled.

PAUSE 2 SECONDS – REPEAT Q.5 – PAUSE 2 SECONDS

6 You hear a radio advertisement. What is being advertised?
   A  package tours
   B  home exchanges
   C  luxury holidays

PAUSE 5 SECONDS

Have you ever wished you could afford luxury holidays abroad? Have you wondered why your friends and neighbours always seem to be packing to go away? Are there parts of the world which you would love to tour? Have you ever wanted another home that's yours for a few weeks every year? If you have, then ring us now on 0099 3126 and find out about our house and apartment swap scheme. We'll send you our brochure and you can choose anywhere in the world. Call us now on 0099 3126 ...

PAUSE 2 SECONDS – REPEAT Q.6 – PAUSE 2 SECONDS

7   **You hear a man talking about why he decided to lose weight. What is the reason he gives?**
    A   He felt overweight.
    B   His clothes were very tight.
    C   He couldn't stop eating.

PAUSE 5 SECONDS

So I took one look at myself and decided, right – that's it. OK, my clothes may still fit me and all that, but I reckon it's how you feel that really matters. And I felt fat. It's no use telling me I don't look fat and that I was never meant to be thin. I mean, some people can eat mountains and never change shape. Me? Well, I don't eat mountains, but there are days when I can't resist the chocolate cake, the ice-cream, the french fries – all the things that are bad for you. I love them!

PAUSE 2 SECONDS – REPEAT Q.7 – PAUSE 2 SECONDS

8   **You overhear two people talking about a woman on their staff. What is the problem?**
    A   She complains all the time.
    B   She gets upset very easily.
    C   She's always late for work.

PAUSE 5 SECONDS

**Woman:** I'm afraid we shall have to talk to her. After all, we did warn her a few months ago that she'd have to change her ways. Get up earlier or leave home earlier.

**Man:** I know. But I think she's likely to get very upset.

**Woman:** That can't be helped. Every day this week she's arrived with some excuse about traffic delays. Everyone else gets here on time and so must she.

**Man:** Oh, yes, you're quite right.

PAUSE 2 SECONDS – REPEAT Q.8 – PAUSE 2 SECONDS

**That is the end of Part 1. Now turn to Part 2.**

## PART 2

**You'll hear a radio interview with a girl called Silvia, who has won a competition. For questions 9-18, complete the sentences. You now have 45 seconds to look at Part 2.**

PAUSE 45 SECONDS

**Interviewer:** Hello, Silvia, welcome to the programme and many congratulations on winning the Young Writer's Award.

**Silvia:** Thank you very much.

**Interviewer:** Now, you're very young, aren't you, to win this prize when you're only seventeen? I mean, the competition is open to people up to the age of twenty-five, so you must be feeling very proud. Is this the first time you've won such a prize?

**Silvia:** Well, actually I have won two other prizes. I won one when I was twelve for a poem which I wrote. That was just a competition run by the local newspaper. And then when I was fourteen I won a short story competition which was organised by Frasers.

**Interviewer:** *The* Frasers? The international booksellers?

**Silvia:** That's right. It meant my story was included with others which had been written by professional writers in a new paperback book, and it was displayed in all their shop windows.

**Interviewer:** So does writing run in your family? Have you always been interested in writing?

**Silvia:** Well, my mother is an engineer and my father surrounded me with pictures – he teaches art – but I suppose they've always encouraged me to read. I remember when I was small, one of them always used to tell me a story before I went to sleep each night. And I just loved listening to those stories. I used to look forward to going to bed. Apparently I never made a fuss about bedtime, but if the story didn't last long enough, I wouldn't let them leave the room until they'd told me some more! And even before I could write properly, I was apparently trying to write stories. Well, they weren't really stories. My mother kept a few of them and they're hilarious. When I look at them now, I can hardly understand a word, but apparently I used to insist that people listened to me whilst I read my own stories aloud.

**Interviewer:** It sounds to me as if you were a born writer ...

**Silvia:** I don't know about that. I just enjoy writing.

**Interviewer:** And do you want to be a professional writer eventually?

**Silvia:** Oh, yes, I do. But I know it's not that easy. Publishing is very competitive and it's very difficult to earn your living by just writing. I especially enjoy writing poetry but it's almost impossible to get poetry published unless you're well known. So when I finish school, I'm hoping to go to university to study psychology. Then if I don't succeed as a writer, I'll be able to develop a career doing something else.

**Interviewer:** Mmm, OK. Now, tell us about the Young Writer's Award and what that is going to mean for you.

**Silvia:** Well, it includes a cheque for a thousand pounds which I'm going to spend on a new computer, but more importantly it means that a publisher will look at some of the things which I've written. I've already met one of the editors from the publishing house and he's going to read some of my work straight away. Also I'm just finishing my first novel and the fact that he will read it is probably the most exciting thing about winning the award. You hear about people who've written novels who get them sent back without anyone ever looking at them seriously. So I feel this is a fantastic opportunity. I don't expect him to say, 'This is a brilliant novel – we'll publish it.' But he'll give me advice on how to improve and develop my writing, and for me that is worth more than any amount of prize money.

PAUSE 10 SECONDS

**Now you'll hear Part 2 again.**

REPEAT PART 2 – PAUSE 5 SECONDS

**That is the end of Part 2. Now turn to Part 3.**

## PART 3

**You'll hear five different people apologising about something. For questions 19-23, choose from the list A-F the reason for each speaker's apology. Use the letters only once. There is one extra letter which you do not need to use. You now have 30 seconds to look at Part 3.**

PAUSE 30 SECONDS

**Speaker 1:**
I'm awfully sorry. I left home in plenty of time and when I got to the bus stop there was a simply enormous queue. Apparently, a bus had broken down earlier and some people had been waiting for up to an hour. I couldn't contact you so I thought you'd just go in and not wait for me. It never occurred to me you'd miss the first act. You should have left a message at the box office because I had to pick up my ticket from there anyway.

PAUSE 5 SECONDS

**Speaker 2:**
The trouble is I'm using two diaries. One for a day-to-day business and the other one for anniversaries and people's birthdays, and so on. You know I've never forgotten before, but when I went away on holiday I was in such a hurry at the last minute that I took the wrong diary with me and I'm really sorry – it just completely slipped my mind. Anyway, I'll make it up to you and we'll go out to a concert or something next week.

PAUSE 5 SECONDS

**Speaker 3:**
I don't understand this. I always make a note of everything. You know, bills, how much I've spent, how much I can save – every month without fail. And it's all recorded in the back of my large desk diary, which I look at every day. I do apologise. It must be the first time this has happened. I hate being in debt. I'll go and get my cheque book this very minute and pay you back now.

PAUSE 5 SECONDS

**Speaker 4:**
I know it was one of your favourites. I'm most terribly sorry. I'll try and find another one which is exactly the same. I've no idea how it happened. It just seemed to slip out of my hands as I was filling it with water. And I bought you these flowers especially to go in that vase and now all I've done is upset you. Please stop crying – I promise I'll get you another one.

PAUSE 5 SECONDS

**Speaker 5:**
I'd no idea it was so late. And in any case I did try and creep in very quietly. I even took my boots off before opening the front door. I don't know what else I could have done. I didn't put on any lights. I tiptoed up the stairs and went straight to bed. I'm extremely sorry you had a sleepless night, but as I say I did my best not to make the slightest noise.

PAUSE 10 SECONDS

**Now you'll hear Part 3 again.**

REPEAT PART 3 – PAUSE 5 SECONDS

**That's the end of Part 3. Now turn to Part 4.**

## PART 4

**You'll hear a conversation which takes place in a café between friends. For questions 24–30, choose the best answer, A, B, or C. You now have one minute to look at Part 4.**

PAUSE 60 SECONDS

**Anna:** Hi, Peter, I'm over here.

**Peter:** Hello, Anna, it's great to see you. Where's Miriam?

**Anna:** She's not here yet. But I know she's coming because she rang me last night.

**Peter:** She was always late for lessons I seem to remember! Anyway, how are things with you? Thanks for the letter by the way, but you didn't say whether you were enjoying your business studies course ...

**Anna:** Oh, I don't know. There's an awful lot of work: we have to do two or three essays a week as well as all the background reading. It's much more difficult than I expected and I'm not sure if it's what I want. It makes school seem like a holiday camp! You know, it feels like ages since we left but it's only six months. Oh, there's Miriam.

**Miriam:** Hi. Oh, I'm sorry I'm a bit late. I missed the bus. Oh, it's really good to see you – just like old times.

**Peter:** How's the job going?

**Miriam:** It's brilliant. What about yours?

**Peter:** Well, I left after a few weeks. It was so boring. At the interview they talked about all the things I would be doing as part of my training and I thought, 'This is just what I want.' But in reality I was stuck in the office all day, sticking stamps on letters, answering the phone, making tea and coffee ...

**Anna:** I know someone else who had a similar experience. What bad luck after looking forward to it as well.

**Peter:** So I'm working for my father at the moment helping in the shop and looking for something else.

**Miriam:** Well, I'm lucky that everything seems to have worked out. The training course is really good and everyone's very friendly and helpful. Every week I go out with one of the reporters from the newspaper and spend a day in court listening to the proceedings and finding out about the different kinds of cases which are worth writing about. Obviously, I don't understand all the legal language but ...

**Anna:** Oh, isn't that really dull? All those judges and things?

**Peter:** It sounds great. I wish I'd thought of doing something like that. I just accepted the first job I was offered without thinking very carefully about it. And now look at me!

**Anna:** Well, it's not too late to change things. I mean, everyone can make mistakes. I think I'll have to decide by the end of this term whether or not I'm going to complete my course. And if I don't, I haven't a clue what to do. My parents are getting really fed up with me.

**Miriam:** I'm sure you'll eventually find something. Look at all those teachers who kept telling me that if I didn't work harder, I'd never get a job. Well, I've proved them wrong, haven't I?

PAUSE 10 SECONDS

**Now you'll hear Part 4 again.**

REPEAT PART 4 – PAUSE 5 SECONDS

**That's the end of Part 4.**

**There'll now be a pause of 5 minutes for you to copy your answers onto the separate answer sheet. Be sure to follow the numbering of all the questions.**

*[In the exam, there will be a pause of 5 minutes. You may wish to stop the recording now. Remind your students when they have one minute left.]*

**That's the end of the test. Please stop now. Your supervisor will now collect all the question papers and answer sheets.**

# PRACTICE TEST 2

**This is the Richmond First Certificate Practice Test Two. Listening. I'm going to give you the instructions for this test. I'll introduce each part of the test and give you time to look at the questions. At the start of each piece you'll hear this sound:**

*Sound effect*

**You'll hear each piece twice.**

**Remember, while you're listening, write your answers on the question paper. You'll have 5 minutes at the end of the test to copy your answers onto the separate answer sheet.**

**There will now be a pause. Please ask any questions now, because you must not speak during the test.**

PAUSE 5 SECONDS

**Now open your question paper and look at Part 1.**

## PART 1

**You'll hear people talking in eight different situations. For questions 1-8, choose the best answer, A, B or C.**

1 **You hear a woman talking on the phone. Who is she talking to?**
   A a store assistant
   B a store manager
   C a store director

PAUSE 5 SECONDS

... but I ordered this over a month ago. And at the time your assistant said that it would take no more than ten days ... Well, I think the advertisement was very misleading. If I'd known it would take so long, I wouldn't have ordered it in the first place ... No, I don't think that's any excuse – it's your job to make sure the goods are in stock ... But the whole point of ordering by phone is to avoid having to come into the store. I've a good mind to write to one of your directors over this ... No, you listen to me ...

PAUSE 2 SECONDS – REPEAT Q.1 – PAUSE 2 SECONDS

2 **You hear a woman talking to a friend. Where has she been?**
   A a music class
   B an exercise class
   C a swimming class     – possible ?

PAUSE 5 SECONDS

Well, I was really nervous about going alone. But then I thought, there are all these other people and they can't possibly all know each other. The first few minutes were awful – while we were waiting for the instructor to come. And then when she arrived, we had to introduce ourselves and that helped break the ice. And then she switched on the CD player and we were off. She made us work non-stop for about 45 minutes – I thought I'd die. I think it's a brilliant way of keeping fit and much better than going on a diet. We can take our own CDs for her to play, so next week I'm going to take one of mine.

PAUSE 2 SECONDS – REPEAT Q.2 – PAUSE 2 SECONDS

**3** You overhear a man talking to his friend. What are they planning to do?
   **A** buy a house in the country
   **B** go away for a holiday
   **C** change where they work

PAUSE 5 SECONDS

**Man:** Have you had a chance to look at those brochures?

**Woman:** Yeah – I liked the one which just covered lakes and mountains.

**Man:** You wouldn't mind not being near a city?

**Woman:** Good gracious no – we spend the whole year travelling in and out of the city for work. It'd be lovely to spend a couple of weeks away from it all.

**Man:** Right then, if you tell me which place you like best, I'll get on and book it.

PAUSE 2 SECONDS – REPEAT Q.3 – PAUSE 2 SECONDS

**4** You hear a radio announcement. What is the next programme about?
   **A** food
   **B** chemistry
   **C** cookery

PAUSE 5 SECONDS

... and that was the last in the series *Cooking is fun*. If you have enjoyed the programmes, you might be interested in listening to the next item which follows shortly. Starting tonight and for the next six weeks, Alan Bowen will be presenting a series on how what we eat affects our moods and behaviour. Professor Bowen believes that food can govern our emotions and that the chemical balances in our body control our behaviour. So if you're thinking of planning next week's menus, stay tuned to this channel.

PAUSE 2 SECONDS – REPEAT Q.4 – PAUSE 2 SECONDS

**5** You overhear a policeman talking to some people. What is about to happen?
   **A** There's going to be a concert.
   **B** There's going to be a parade.
   **C** There's going to be a match.

PAUSE 5 SECONDS

Keep moving, please. There'll be more room for everyone if you keep moving. Let the little ones stand in the front or they'll never see anything. Once the barriers go up, you won't be able to cross the road. You'll have to wait until the end of the procession before you can leave the area, so don't get stuck in the crowd if you should be somewhere else. No pushing and shoving if you please – this isn't a game of football. Watch your bags please, keep moving. Not long to wait now – you can hear the band in the distance.

PAUSE 2 SECONDS – REPEAT Q.5 – PAUSE 2 SECONDS

**6** You hear a man telling someone about a recent experience in a theatre. What had happened?
   **A** His seat broke during the performance.
   **B** He was given a free seat for the show.
   **C** His seat was broken when he arrived.

PAUSE 5 SECONDS

I simply couldn't believe it. It was about five minutes before the performance was due to start and I hadn't even tried to sit down. So I actually picked up the seat and went back to the guy who was taking the tickets on the door. His eyes popped out of his head when I handed him the seat and a handful of screws! But he was very good. 'Follow me, sir,' he said. 'I do apologise for this.' And before I knew it, he'd taken me to the front of the circle and offered me a seat which is normally reserved for guests of the director.

PAUSE 2 SECONDS – REPEAT Q.6 – PAUSE 2 SECONDS

**7** You hear a woman explaining why she is late. What is the reason she gives?
   **A** Two trains were withdrawn.
   **B** The drivers were on strike.
   **C** She missed her first train.

PAUSE 5 SECONDS

Yes, of course I left in plenty of time. I was on the platform at least ten minutes before the train was due. And then there was an announcement saying that the next train had been cancelled as there was a shortage of drivers. As if that wasn't bad enough! We waited half an hour for the next train, and when that was due we were told it had broken down and had been taken out of service. Do you know that in the end I must have waited about an hour and half? I can tell you I almost went home I was so fed up.

PAUSE 2 SECONDS – REPEAT Q.7 – PAUSE 2 SECONDS

**8** You hear two people talking about their work. What kind of work do they do?
   **A** They make bread.
   **B** They work in a hospital.
   **C** They clean offices.

PAUSE 5 SECONDS

**Man 1:** Well, I know people complain, but I reckon we're lucky to have a job these days.

**Man 2:** But I do hate getting up early in the mornings. When I tell people I have to get up at five o'clock each day, they're horrified. It's worse than working in a bakery or being a night nurse.

**Man 1:** You've got to remember that we've finished by midday and the rest of the day is ours. And we can do the floors and the furniture before anyone starts work and nobody pushes us around telling us what to do. I like polishing all those desks and leaving everything nice and bright.

**Man 2:** Yes, I suppose so.

PAUSE 2 SECONDS – REPEAT Q.8 – PAUSE 2 SECONDS

**That's the end of Part 1. Now turn to Part 2.**

## PART 2

You'll hear a travel company representative called Samantha talking to some hotel guests at the start of their holiday. For questions 9-18, complete the sentences. You now have 45 seconds to look at Part 2.

PAUSE 45 SECONDS

Good morning, my name's Samantha and I'm here to welcome you on behalf of Panorama Tours. I hope you all had a comfortable flight and you're not feeling too jet-lagged. I've prepared a fact sheet for you – there's a copy for each of you – but before I give them out there are just a few things I'd like to add. There'll be time at the end to ask any questions, so please do ask if there's anything else you'd like to know.

Right. Now I'm available every day from nine in the morning for a couple of hours. You can find me in the same office as the hotel porter. If you can't reach me at the office and it's an emergency, then get in touch with the hotel reception desk. But I do stress that it has to be really urgent before the hotel will use my mobile number. If it's a question of illness, then you should consult the hotel doctor, who will advise you what to do.

There are various excursions organised by Panorama Tours which you might like to book. These are listed on your fact sheet. Payment must be made at the time of booking, and in order to reserve a place on the coach you must book at least 24 hours in advance. I can particularly recommend the tour to Mount Sispi, the volcanic mountain. This is a whole day tour but well worth it. The views from the top are spectacular but it can get very cold up there so do remember to bring some warm clothing with you.

Now, on to the immediate question of where to eat as your hotel only provides breakfast. There are a number of very good local restaurants which you'll find in the town centre. At the bottom of the fact sheet you'll find a list of names and addresses. If you tell the restaurant staff that you're on holiday with Panorama Tours, then you will be offered a ten per cent reduction on your meal. All you need to do is to show them this fact sheet and give them your name.

If you plan on shopping, then shops don't open until quite late in the morning – anything between ten and eleven – but they also stay open until late at night. It's not unusual to find shops still open at midnight, especially small family-run businesses. However, banks and post offices close early so don't get caught out as changing money is best done through a bank. If you do run short of cash, most stores will accept credit cards but there is an additional charge for the service.

Another thing which some tourists are not prepared for are the strict traffic rules. You must cross the road at pedestrian crossings and not at any other point. If you disobey this rule and you are spotted by the traffic police, then you will be fined – usually on the spot! So don't get impatient or it will cost you.

And finally a word of warning about taxis. Only official taxis are allowed to display a special licence plate on the front and back of the vehicle. There have been a number of reports recently of taxis ...

PAUSE 10 SECONDS

Now you'll hear Part 2 again.

REPEAT PART 2 – PAUSE 5 SECONDS

That is the end of Part 2. Now turn to Part 3.

## PART 3

You'll hear five different people talking about being the eldest child in a family. For questions 19-23, choose from the list A-F the best thing each speaker remembers about being the eldest. Use the letters only once. There is one extra letter which you do not need to use. You now have 30 seconds to look at Part 3.

PAUSE 30 SECONDS

**Speaker 1:**
To be honest, I don't remember being jealous of my brother and sister. I think I always expected to come first and I must have been in my late teens – around 17 or 18 – before it occurred to me that my parents had to divide their time amongst the three of us. And I suppose I felt irritated rather than jealous. I remember arguments about having to wait my turn. But my sister wasn't born until I was almost six, so for the first few years of my life I had my parents all to myself and I think that experience was very special and I'm really glad I was born first.

PAUSE 5 SECONDS

**Speaker 2:**
I know our parents tried to treat us all the same, but I remember my younger brother and sister complaining about having to wear my second-hand jeans or trainers. And of course, being the eldest, there was nothing my parents could hand on to me and say, 'Right, you don't need a new sweater – or whatever – you can wear John's old one.' In that respect, I think the eldest child's very lucky.

PAUSE 5 SECONDS

**Speaker 3:**
I used to love those little privileges. You know, when you were allowed to stay up late and the younger ones had to go to bed early. Or if my parents had friends round for a meal and I was allowed to join them. Looking back now, I imagine I must have been a horrible older brother. I don't think it ever occurred to me to ask my parents to let my sisters share in some of the little treats. I was only too pleased to have them all to myself. I must have been a very selfish child.

PAUSE 5 SECONDS

**Speaker 4:**
I clearly remember wanting to know if my parents liked me best. I used to look after my younger brother and sister and hope that my parents would be pleased with me. I think I hoped that they would favour me above the younger children. I enjoyed pleasing them and having that feeling of satisfaction. And this early role of taking care of others is probably one of the reasons why I enjoy taking responsibility for things that need doing and being a caring person generally.

PAUSE 5 SECONDS

**Speaker 5:**

I think my parents were so busy looking after my younger brothers and sisters that I was given quite a lot of freedom. So I became independent at a very early age and went off at weekends and did my own thing. I used to disappear for the whole day with my friends – cycling, camping, canoeing – and although I didn't realise it at the time, I developed a confidence in being able to look after myself. So, I wasn't the least bit worried about moving away from home and living by myself.

PAUSE 10 SECONDS

**Now you'll hear Part 3 again.**

REPEAT PART 3 – PAUSE 5 SECONDS

**That's the end of Part 3. Now turn to Part 4.**

## PART 4

**You'll hear part of an interview with two young people, Mariko and Ronan. For questions 24-30, choose the best answer, A, B or C. You now have one minute to look at Part 4.**

PAUSE 60 SECONDS

**Presenter:** ... and welcome to *The Dreamers*, a weekly programme in which we talk to young people who have fulfilled their dreams. In the studio with me this week are Mariko who's always wanted to be a model and Ronan who has achieved his ambition of running his own business. Mariko, let me ask you first of all – how did this dream come true? I mean, six months ago you were working in a supermarket!

**Mariko:** That's right. I know it sounds unbelievable. But while I was at work one day, a woman came in and gave me her business card. She worked for an agency and said that she thought I'd make a really good model. So I went along and they took some photos of me and sent them off to another agency in London – one of the really big agencies, you know. Well, I waited weeks and didn't hear anything and then one day I got a phone call and this guy said, 'We can use you but you'll have to move to London.' Well, my parents weren't very keen on the idea but they agreed I could try. So the agency booked me into a small hotel in central London, but after that it was terrible.

**Presenter:** In what way?

**Mariko:** The agency simply gives you a list of possible jobs and tells you to buy a map.

**Presenter:** So it's just left to you? Nobody goes with you?

**Mariko:** No. You take your photgraphs with you and you sit there with all the other models while somebody looks through your photos and then you go off and hope someone will ring you and tell you you've got the job.

**Presenter:** And did you have to wait long?

**Mariko:** About three weeks, which isn't long at all really, but at the time it seemed like years. I was terribly lonely.

**Presenter:** And what was your first job?

**Mariko:** It was a small photo to illustrate a letter which had been sent to the problem page of a girls' magazine. I was meant to be the writer of the letter!

**Presenter:** And since then?

**Mariko:** Oh, it's been brilliant. I've had loads of work, even some modelling jobs abroad. And next year looks even better. My diary is already quite full.

**Presenter:** Now Ronan, tell us what you dreamt about?

**Ronan:** Well, basically I wanted to be my own boss. When I left school my parents wanted me to go to college but I didn't want to.

**Presenter:** Why not?

**Ronan:** I don't know. I just knew that I wanted to be out working and not studying. But I couldn't get a job and for the first three months it was desperate. And then one morning I was doing the shopping for my mum – I think it was at the beginning of November – and I was in this shop in the town where we live when a chap came in and said to the shopkeeper that he wouldn't be able to start putting up the Christmas decorations ...

**Presenter:** Christmas decorations?

**Ronan:** Yeah, coloured lights and things across the streets.

**Presenter:** Oh, right.

**Ronan:** ... because the boy who worked with him was ill and he couldn't do it alone as it was too dangerous without someone holding the ladder. And without even thinking what I was doing I said, 'I'll help you.' And he said, 'Great, come on then.' So that was it. I spent the next eight weeks working with him and putting up all these lights and Christmas trees and decorations – not just in our town but in the surrounding towns as well.

**Presenter:** And then?

**Ronan:** Well, after the holiday we took them all down again! And I thought that was going to be the end of it. But it's a full-time business. All the lights and wiring have to be checked and then people hire some of the equipment for parties, barbecues, festivals, and so on. But he wasn't interested in carrying on with the business – he'd had enough – and he asked me if I'd like to take it over. Apparently, his son had emigrated so he couldn't pass it on. And it was just the chance I'd wanted.

PAUSE 10 SECONDS

**Now you'll hear Part 4 again.**

REPEAT PART 4 – PAUSE 5 SECONDS

That's the end of Part 4.

There'll now be a pause of 5 minutes for you to copy your answers onto the separate answer sheet. Be sure to follow the numbering of all the questions.

*[In the exam, there will be a pause of 5 minutes. You may wish to stop the recording now. Remind your students when they have one minute left.]*

That's the end of the test. Please stop now. Your supervisor will now collect all the question papers and answer sheets.

# PRACTICE TEST 3

This is the Richmond First Certificate Practice Test Three. Listening. I'm going to give you the instructions for this test. I'll introduce each part of the test and give you time to look at the questions. At the start of each piece you'll hear this sound:

*Sound effect*

You'll hear each piece twice.

Remember while you're listening, write your answers on the question paper. You'll have 5 minutes at the end of the test to copy your answers onto the separate answer sheet.

There'll now be a pause. Please ask any questions now, because you must not speak during the test.

PAUSE 5 SECONDS

Now open your question paper and look at Part 1.

### PART 1

You'll hear people talking in eight different situations. For questions 1-8, choose the best answer, A, B or C.

1   You are being shown around a factory. What is the speaker talking about?
    A   wood
    B   diamonds
    C   steel

*testing knowledge? word knowledge?*

PAUSE 5 SECONDS

... now if you look very carefully, you'll see that the craftsman is using a very soft cloth for polishing. This is the final stage in the process, which makes the stone shine and gives it its natural beauty. Unlike metal, the final product reflects a whole range of different colours depending on the light.

PAUSE 2 SECONDS – REPEAT Q.1 – PAUSE 2 SECONDS

2   You hear a boy talking. Why is he upset?
    A   He lost his wallet.
    B   He missed his train.
    C   He bought the wrong ticket.

PAUSE 5 SECONDS

I had about three minutes left to get my ticket and I put my hand in my pocket and you know what – right, of course, my wallet wasn't there. So I said, 'Can I buy my ticket on the

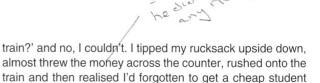

*I thought he didn't have any money?*

train?' and no, I couldn't. I tipped my rucksack upside down, almost threw the money across the counter, rushed onto the train and then realised I'd forgotten to get a cheap student return. So the whole journey cost me twice as much.

PAUSE 2 SECONDS – REPEAT Q.2 – PAUSE 2 SECONDS

3   You hear two students discussing a party they've been to. What did they think of it?
    A   It was very noisy.
    B   It was very boring. – *rooted?*
    C   It was very crowded.

PAUSE 5 SECONDS

**Woman:**  I thought the music was brilliant and just the right number of people for dancing, not so many you kept bumping into each other.

**Man:**  Yeah, but I'm not surprised the neighbours complained – the music was terribly loud.

**Woman:**  I know, you could hear it at the end of the street even when the windows were closed!

PAUSE 2 SECONDS – REPEAT Q.3 – PAUSE 2 SECONDS

4   You overhear a man talking to a customer in a shop. What is he suggesting?
    A   The customer should try another shop.
    B   One of the new coats might suit her.
    C   Last season's colours were nicer.

*A+C are unlikely*

PAUSE 5 SECONDS

I think you'll find that most of our new stock is in this season's colours, madam. You're quite right – we did have the coat you're looking for last year but you will appreciate that both the style and the colours have changed this year. You might like to consider trying on one of the coats in our latest range as you haven't been able to find what you want anywhere else.

PAUSE 2 SECONDS – REPEAT Q.4 – PAUSE 2 SECONDS

5   You overhear a photographer talking about some pictures she's taken. What does she say about the results?
    A   The colours are far too bright.
    B   The prints are not light enough.
    C   The photos are disappointing.

*out of date?*

PAUSE 5 SECONDS

**Woman:**  I spent ages waiting for the sun to go down as I wanted the light to be exactly right. I'd seen such beautiful sunsets and I knew that you had to be very patient – which I was. The effect of that lovely warm glow probably only lasts a few minutes. So I was really surprised when I collected the prints to discover that my patience had been completely wasted and the effect was missing.

PAUSE 2 SECONDS – REPEAT Q.5 – PAUSE 2 SECONDS

6   You hear a mother talking to her child. What has he done?
    A   lost his jumper
    B   broken his leg
    C   hurt his knee

PAUSE 5 SECONDS

I told you not to play football near that rose bush. You've torn your jumper and broken some of the roses. Look at your leg. It's covered in scratches – and what have you done to your knee? You'd better put a plaster on it.

PAUSE 2 SECONDS – REPEAT Q.6 – PAUSE 2 SECONDS

**7   Your friend is using your phone. Who is she speaking to?**
  **A   a doctor's receptionist**
  **B   a hospital receptionist**
  **C   a dental receptionist**

*could be any of three different ... different countries*

PAUSE 5 SECONDS

Well, I'd like an appointment as soon as possible, please. ... No, it's not an emergency, but it's very difficult to swallow because I can't chew things properly and my throat is really sore. I think it's because I can't bite on the right hand side since the filling came out, and the tooth is quite loose. ... Yes, I can come any time today.

PAUSE 2 SECONDS – REPEAT Q.7 – PAUSE 2 SECONDS

**8   You hear two people talking about a journey. What is the problem?**
  **A   There are no trains.**
  **B   The roads are very busy.**
  **C   The bus drivers are on strike.**

PAUSE 5 SECONDS

**Woman 1:**   Well, usually I would expect to go by train but with the strike on there are only a few trains running.

**Woman 2:**   We could go by bus or car.

**Woman 1:**   It would take a long time to get through the traffic, and we'd never find anywhere to park.

**Woman 2:**   Then I think we'd better postpone the meeting until things are back to normal.

PAUSE 2 SECONDS – REPEAT Q.8 – PAUSE 2 SECONDS

**That's the end of Part 1. Now turn to Part 2.**

*all / most contexts ✓*

*negative*

*v. depressing*

1 B        5 C
2 C        6 B
3 A        7 C
4 A        8 B

---

**You'll hear a radio interview with a young man called Iain, who has just spent a year in Russia. For questions 9-18, complete the sentences. You now have 45 seconds to look at Part 2.**

PAUSE 45 SECONDS

**Interviewer:**   Hello. In the studio with me today is Iain Searle, who has just returned from a year in Russia. Iain – welcome back!

**Iain:**   Thank you.

**Interviewer:**   Iain, why Russia? Or more precisely, why Siberia?

**Iain:**   Well, it was somewhere I'd always wanted to visit. I don't know why – certainly not for the weather!

**Interviewer:**   Was it very cold?

**Iain:**   Not all the time obviously, but in the depths of winter, yes, it was freezing. But when I arrived in July, I was in St Petersburg for the first couple of weeks at a student centre, and the weather was warm and sunny. There were lots of students from all over the world at the centre attending this programme which is called an orientation programme.

**Interviewer:**   Did you speak Russian?

**Iain:**   I didn't when I went, but I do now! But the orientation programme was in English and we learnt about Russian customs, the transport system, shopping, where to change money, the food – the sort of things that make everyday survival possible. Then I went on to Omsk to an international student conference and when we landed *there*, then I knew we'd arrived in Siberia. It was August and a chilly 7 degrees. The conference was organised and attended by students from across Siberia and it was really enjoyable. By then I was beginning to pick up a little of the language, and everyone was very kind and friendly.

**Interviewer:**   And after Omsk?

**Iain:**   The next part was brilliant. I travelled on the Trans-Siberian railway to Novosibirsk, which was something I'd always wanted to do. I love travelling by rail and I met so many interesting people who always wanted to try out their English. So I'd listen to them speak English and then I'd practise my Russian on them. Apparently, Novosibirsk owes its existence to the railway. In appearance it's quite a grey place and it's a complete contrast to St Petersburg. But it has a population of one and a half million and is a very busy city. It's got an extensive public transport system with buses, trams, trolley buses and even a small metro, an underground railway. There are a few outside markets and generally a lot of street stalls everywhere selling bread, vegetables, sweets, clothes, and so on.

**Interviewer:** And did you manage to get a job during your time there?

**Iain:** Yes, I did, fortunately, otherwise I wouldn't have been able to stay. Well, not an official job because I would have needed a work permit to work full-time. But I found a school which taught Russian. And I decided I could afford two lessons a day – about two hours. My teacher was excellent although I didn't find it a particularly easy language to learn. Anyway, we got on very well together and he suggested that I should give English conversation lessons in order to earn some money. He knew of students who were anxious to have conversation lessons with an English speaker, and so in fact I ended up with fourteen students!

**Interviewer:** How amazing!

**Iain:** Yes, I didn't have to advertise and if I'd wanted to take more students, then I could have done. I also organised 'English suppers' when everyone would come round to my flat and I'd try and cook something typically English – with varying degrees of success, I might add! I phoned my mother and she sent out some simple recipes, so I've become a much better cook in the process. But the main thing was that everyone had to speak English, as the whole point was to improve their English, not to eat my dreadful cooking!

**Interviewer:** I'm sure it wasn't dreadful. And did you spend the rest of the year in Novosibirsk?

**Iain:** No. I travelled on to Irkutsk – when I eventually got a visa – and joined up with some friends from the conference in Omsk and ...

PAUSE 10 SECONDS

**Now you'll hear Part 2 again.**

REPEAT PART 2 – PAUSE 5 SECONDS

**That's the end of Part 2. Now turn to Part 3.**

## PART 3

**You'll hear five different people talking about jobs. For questions 19-23, choose from the list A-F the job each speaker is describing. Use the letters only once. There is one extra letter which you do not need to use. You now have 30 seconds to look at Part 3.**

PAUSE 30 SECONDS
**Speaker 1:**
What really impressed me about him was the incredibly long hours that he was prepared to work. And it wasn't as if he earned loads of money either. In fact, I think there were times when he had to struggle – particularly when the children were young. It meant getting up very early in the morning, which in winter must have been pretty disagreeable, and working quite late at night if there were any problems. And then if the weather was awful, it could affect the crop so badly that of course your income suffered. He may have spent three years at college, but they don't teach you what

to do about controlling the weather, do they?

PAUSE 5 SECONDS
**Speaker 2:**
I can see the attraction of not working for an employer and in being your own boss, but I wouldn't fancy the insecurity. You know, waiting for the phone to ring, wondering if anyone's ever going to ask you to do anything ever again. And then hoping your work will be noticed, that someone will see something that you've done hanging on a wall and say, 'Oh, where did you get that?' And so your name gets mentioned. Or even worse, dragging your stuff around various galleries, watching the owners look through it and finally say, 'No, sorry. Not quite what our customers like.'

PAUSE 5 SECONDS
**Speaker 3:**
I suppose years ago a university degree was a passport to almost any job, but I'm not so sure now. Most employers want experience these days before you can get anything worthwhile. So I can understand why she's attracted to education and there always seem to be plenty of jobs going. There'll always be kids. And although I wish she'd gone on to study medicine – it's much better paid – if that's what she wants to do, then who am I to say no? But it's going to be quite a tough life.

PAUSE 5 SECONDS
**Speaker 4:**
I remember being quite envious of people like her. I had friends whose parents were in the business and got to travel all over the world. It seemed very glamorous, but I guess it must get quite exhausting. Constantly packing and unpacking, loading up all your gear and maybe staying every night in a different place. If you want to get married and have a family, it must be really difficult. But then she's so good and audiences love her.

PAUSE 5 SECONDS
**Speaker 5:**
It's a good life if you're successful, but then that applies to most things. But I think it must be hard work building up the business in the early years. You've got to be willing to work all hours and do whatever's necessary. I know someone whose staff were always letting him down and never turning up on time. I think at one stage he almost gave up – he was doing everything single-handed. It's very different now of course. He's a big name. Hardly ever goes near a hot stove, although he's the brains behind some of the most imaginative dishes.

PAUSE 10 SECONDS

**Now you'll hear Part 3 again.**

REPEAT PART 3 – PAUSE 5 SECONDS

**That's the end of Part 3. Now turn to Part 4.**

## PART 4

You will hear part of a radio programme in which a girl called Sasha Lombard is interviewed about her part in a recent film. For questions 24–30, choose the best answer, A, B or C. You now have one minute to look at Part 4.

PAUSE 1 MINUTE

**Interviewer:** In the studio with me today is Sasha Lombard who recently starred in the film *Altogether Now*. Sasha, welcome to the programme.

**Sasha:** Hey, thanks for inviting me.

**Interviewer:** I suppose what we all want to know is how you got involved in the film in the first place.

**Sasha:** Right! Well, it's quite weird, really. One of the subjects I study at school is Drama – you know Theatre Arts – and the guy who teaches us, Mr Theo, used to be on the stage. So, obviously he knew lots of people in the acting world – agents, producers, directors and so on. And one day, at the end of the lesson, he said, 'By the way, Joel Brookes is coming to the school next week.' And we're like 'What? *The* Joel Brookes', cos as you know he's dead famous.

**Interviewer:** Absolutely! So why was he visiting your school?

**Sasha:** Well, the producer of *Altogether Now* was looking for a suitable school which they could use for some of the scenes in the film. And so he'd contacted our Theatre Arts teacher because they'd worked together years ago and had remained friends. And he asked if he could bring Joel Brookes with him as he was playing the lead role in the film, although Mr Theo had never met him.

**Interviewer:** Right -

**Sasha:** Anyway, when the producer and Joel turned up we were in the middle of a drama lesson with our teacher and they asked if they could sit through the lesson. It was so embarrassing, I mean we couldn't stop looking at Joel Brookes – he's so gorgeous! In the end, Mr Theo stopped the lesson because we couldn't concentrate and we all just had a chat and got Joel Brookes' autograph, of course!

**Interviewer:** And after that?

**Sasha:** Well, that was it. We all went off to our next lesson. I saw him in the school canteen at lunch time, but he didn't see me, and in any case he was surrounded by loads of other kids watching him eat! And by this time, there were loads of people hanging around outside the school because word had got around that Joel Brookes was in town.

**Interviewer:** So what happened next?

**Sasha:** At the end of the school day, Mr Theo asked to see me. I thought it was because I'd been messing around and laughing in his drama lesson and he was going to tell me off. But when I got to his room, Joel Brookes and the producer were sitting there. Mr Theo explained that they were looking for someone to play the role of a 16 year old school girl and they wanted me to do a screen test. I couldn't believe it!

**Interviewer:** What did your parents say?

**Sasha:** Well, to begin with they weren't very keen because they thought I'd miss a lot of school and it would affect my exam results. So, although I missed a couple of days because I had to go to the studios in London, when I actually got the part I was given my own private teacher who had been hired by the film company. So in the end, they were very supportive.

**Interviewer:** But weren't they filming at your school anyway?

**Sasha:** Yeah, but only outdoor shots. When it came to classroom scenes and other interior shots, those were filmed in the studios. And by law, all children have to continue with their education. So in between shooting, I had lessons in all my subjects. And at times, it was really annoying because I wanted to stay and watch Joel Brookes and the other actors. But it was an opportunity my friends would've killed for, so I can't complain.

**Interviewer:** Yes, I can imagine how frustrating that must've been for them. Anyway, let's go on to the night of the film premiere and ... [FADE]

PAUSE 10 SECONDS

**Now you'll hear Part 4 again.**

REPEAT PART 4 – PAUSE 5 SECONDS

**That's the end of Part 4.**

**There'll now be a pause of 5 minutes for you to copy your answers onto the separate answer sheet. Be sure to follow the numbering of all the questions.**

*[In the exam, there will be a pause of 5 minutes. You may wish to stop the recording now. Remind your students when they have one minute left.]*

**That's the end of the test. Please stop now. Your supervisor will now collect all the question papers and answer sheets.**

# PRACTICE TEST 4

This is the Richmond First Certificate Practice Test Four. Listening. I'm going to give you the instructions for this test. I'll introduce each part of the test and give you time to look at the questions. At the start of each piece you'll hear this sound:

*Sound effect*

**You'll hear each piece twice.**

**Remember, while you're listening, write your answers on the question paper. You'll have time at the end of the test to copy your answers onto the separate answer sheet.**

**There'll now be a pause. Please ask any questions now, because you must not speak during the test.**

PAUSE 5 SECONDS

**Now open your question paper and look at Part 1.**

## PART 1

You'll hear people talking in eight different situations. For questions 1-8, choose the best answer, A, B or C.

1  You hear a hotel guest complaining to the manager of the hotel. What is he complaining about?
   A  the phone in his room
   B  the TV in his room
   C  the safe in his room

PAUSE 5 SECONDS

So, although I have closed it, I can't open it again. I've tried dialling the number – in fact I've done that at least three times in exactly the way the picture on the front shows you how to. And I can hear the buzzing noise as I press each number, but when I push the button, the door won't open. It's extremely inconvenient because the tickets for tonight's concert are inside. I'd be very grateful if you could send one of your staff to fix it. Thank you very much.

PAUSE 2 SECONDS – REPEAT Q.1 – PAUSE 2 SECONDS

2  You hear a woman asking about her missing glasses. Where does she think she left them?
   A  with some magazines
   B  in her hand luggage
   C  on her aircraft seat

PAUSE 5 SECONDS

Hello, is that the airline lost property desk? ... Oh good. Yes, I've just arrived from London on flight SY 303 and I'm afraid I've left my glasses on board the plane. ... My seat number? Just a minute, um, 47G. ... No, I don't think I left them on the seat as I would have seen them. I had some hand luggage in the overhead locker, but they certainly weren't in my luggage as I had them during the flight. I think they may have got folded up inside all the flight magazines when I put them back.

PAUSE 2 SECONDS – REPEAT Q.2 – PAUSE 2 SECONDS

3  You overhear two students discussing some arrangements. What is the problem?
   A  The concert has been cancelled.
   B  The trip to the coast is too expensive.
   C  Two events are on the same day.

PAUSE 5 SECONDS

**Man:**  It's a pity about having to cancel the excursion to the coast next Saturday.

**Woman:**  Yeah, I know, but only six people signed up to go, and you need at least twenty-five before you can hire a coach – otherwise it costs a fortune.

**Man:**  Yet when we were talking about it, over thirty people said they were interested.

**Woman:**  Well, apparently there's a concert on that night and we wouldn't get back in time for the start of it.

**Man:**  Well, I'm really disappointed as I'd been looking forward to it.

PAUSE 2 SECONDS – REPEAT Q.3 – PAUSE 2 SECONDS

4  You hear a radio announcement. What is the warning about?
   A  damaged bridges
   B  violent weather
   C  delayed departures

PAUSE 5 SECONDS

... and the high winds which have been sweeping across the country have begun to die down. There are reports of damage to buildings and bridges although no one has been injured. However, storms and heavy rain are expected in the next 24 hours, and drivers are advised not to make any unnecessary journeys. Although most flights are leaving on time, incoming flights are up to three hours late in some cases, so if you're planning on meeting people ...

PAUSE 2 SECONDS – REPEAT Q.4 – PAUSE 2 SECONDS

5  You overhear a tour guide talking to some people. Where are they going?
   A  on a mountain tour
   B  on an island tour
   C  on a factory tour

PAUSE 5 SECONDS

... and a warm welcome to you all. I'm afraid we have to make a slight alteration to today's tour. We would normally take you to the top of the mountain so you could enjoy the views. But as you will see from the fog and mist this morning, such a journey would be pointless. We will still be taking you around the island and the surrounding countryside, but at the end of the morning we shall stop at a factory where they process cocoa beans. This is a famous factory where you can buy different kinds of chocolate at very cheap prices, much cheaper than you would normally pay in the shops.

PAUSE 2 SECONDS – REPEAT Q.5 – PAUSE 2 SECONDS

**6** You overhear two girls talking about a road accident. What happened to Linda?
  A  She ran into a line of parked cars.
  B  She was knocked down by a car.
  C  She fell over right in front of a taxi.

PAUSE 5 SECONDS

**Girl 1:** No, she's fine – a bit shocked but that's only natural.

**Girl 2:** It's a good job there wasn't very much traffic.

**Girl 1:** Well, there was, but it was at a junction and so the cars were waiting to pull out onto the main road. And Linda went running across the road thinking it was a one-way street. So she didn't even see the taxi coming round the corner, but fortunately the taxi driver was going quite slowly so he managed to brake.

**Girl 2:** So, how was she hurt if he braked in time?

**Girl 1:** I think she tripped over very heavily and that's why her legs are covered in bruises.

PAUSE 2 SECONDS – REPEAT Q. 6 – PAUSE 2 SECONDS

**7** You hear a man talking. What is he talking about?
  A  finding a lot of money
  B  counting a lot of money
  C  winning a lot of money

PAUSE 5 SECONDS

I was walking past the sports centre when I saw it on the ground so of course I picked it up. It was full of money. I didn't count it, but it was a thick bundle of notes as if someone had won it. So I looked for a name and address so I could return it to whoever had dropped it. Well, there were some photos inside and some old bus tickets, but absolutely nothing to say who it belonged to. So I went into the sports centre and there was this woman at the desk in tears, explaining she'd lost something. I've never seen anyone look so happy. She actually threw her arms round me and kissed me. It was quite embarrassing really!

PAUSE 2 SECONDS – REPEAT Q.7 – PAUSE 2 SECONDS

**8** You hear a brother and sister talking together. What are they discussing?
  A  a present for a sick relative
  B  a special birthday present
  C  a present for an anniversary

PAUSE 5 SECONDS

**Boy:** So if I buy Mum some flowers, will you get her a vase?

**Girl:** She's got plenty of vases. Can't we think of something more original?

**Boy:** But she loves flowers ...

**Girl:** Yeah, but it ought to be something different. She's going to be fifty so it's not just an ordinary occasion. And we took her flowers when she was in hospital last month. And Dad gave her some jewellery to celebrate their wedding anniversary. Let's get her a picture or a painting, something small but original.

PAUSE 2 SECONDS – REPEAT Q.8 – PAUSE 2 SECONDS

**That's the end of Part 1. Now turn to Part 2.**

**PART 2**

You'll hear a man who has just flown in from abroad being interviewed about the airport's facilities. For questions 9-18, complete the sentences. You now have 45 seconds to look at Part 2.

PAUSE 45 SECONDS

**Interviewer:** Excuse me, sir, I wonder if you could spare a few minutes to answer some questions?

**Passenger:** Oh, right, OK then, I've got half an hour before my train leaves. What's it to do with?

**Interviewer:** I'm carrying out a survey on behalf of the airlines which use this airport. As you probably know, there are plans to develop a new terminal in the future. Could I ask you first which country you've just flown in from?

**Passenger:** I've been down under, Australia to you, but I broke my journey in India and spent two nights there if ...

**Interviewer:** No, I meant your main departure. And have you been working or on holiday?

**Passenger:** Well, to be honest I was there on behalf of my firm but I managed to fit in a few days on the beach.

**Interviewer:** Right, so you were working. And did you leave your car at the airport?

**Passenger:** You've got to be joking! At the prices they charge for the car park? It'd cost me a fortune to leave the car here for three weeks. No way. As I said – I've got a train to catch in half an hour.

**Interviewer:** Right. Next question. If the car park charges were lower, would you prefer to come by car?

**Passenger:** Oh, is that what they're planning? Well, I don't rightly know. I don't suppose I would really. If you look at all those jams on the motorway, I think I'd rather come by public transport. Mind you, I don't rate the train that highly with all the delays there seem to be. I think I'd rather use the bus or one of those coach services which drop you off outside the entrance. But where I come from, there isn't a direct service.

**Interviewer:** OK. Now, could I ask you about the check-in facilities? How long did you have to spend queuing in order to check in?

**Passenger:** Far too long, I can tell you. I don't know – they tell you to get here at least two hours before your flight leaves, and what happens? You spend almost an hour just standing ...

**Interviewer:** So you spent an hour waiting to check in?

**Passenger:** Well, I suppose it's a bit of an exaggeration, but at least three quarters of an hour.

**Interviewer:** And what about the baggage reclaim just now when you collected your luggage?

**Passenger:** Now there I was pleasantly surprised – for once. I usually have to hang around for hours but getting in this early – I mean, it's not seven o'clock yet, is it? – I was only delayed for about twenty minutes. Now that's what I like.

**Interviewer:** Right. Now the last few questions are concerned with refreshment and shopping facilities. Generally speaking, what kind of refreshment facilities do you require? For example, do you like to have a complete meal, a drink or a snack, or do you prefer to wait until you've boarded your plane?

**Passenger:** Well, I never say no to food – I can tell you that! It's a lonely life travelling around but you can usually find someone to talk to in a café or a restaurant. But I don't think people want big meals when they're flying, so I reckon you need a self-service place where you can help yourself and then something like a snack bar if you haven't got much time. Cetainly not a restaurant, where you might have to wait ages to be served.

**Interviewer:** And the last question. Shopping. With the exception of the duty-free and the things that are sold there like perfume, alcohol, cigarettes, and so on, are there any particular shops which you always make a point of visiting even if you don't buy anything?

**Passenger:** Well, I'd like to try out all the aftershaves and perfumes, but my wife would never speak to me again if I didn't go to the shop which sells her favourite chocolates. And although I can't say I've ever bought anything, I always go and have a look at that, er, that posh shoe shop. Can't afford anything but their leather stuff is the best I've ever seen. Imported from South America I think.

**Interviewer:** Thank you very much, sir. I hope you have a pleasant journey home.

**Passenger:** Oh, right, that's it, is it? And there I was ...

PAUSE 10 SECONDS

**Now you'll hear Part 2 again.**

REPEAT PART 2 – PAUSE 5 SECONDS

**That's the end of Part 2. Now turn to Part 3.**

*Most ace from elderly perspech*

## PART 3

**You'll hear five different people talking about things they miss. For questions 19-23, choose from the list A-F the thing each person misses. Use the letters only once. There is one extra letter which you do not need to use. You now have 30 seconds to look at Part 3.**

PAUSE 30 SECONDS

**Speaker 1:**

Well, when my parents moved house, we moved from living in the country to living in a city. And I remember waking up the first morning in the new house, and looking out of my bedroom window and being horrified by how close the roofs of all the other houses were. I'd been used to looking out at fields and hills and I felt so closed in by all the buildings. I don't know how people can bear to live surrounded by row upon row of houses.

PAUSE 5 SECONDS

**Speaker 2:**

When I first lived abroad, I thought it was wonderful. Well, I suppose I still do otherwise I wouldn't be here. But one of the things I've never got used to is having to go without some of life's little pleasures. It sounds silly really. I love cheese, and the only cheese you can get here is in tins, and it tastes nothing like the real thing. At times I think I can almost feel the texture and see the yellow creamy colour and then I can almost smell it, that ripe sharp smell.

PAUSE 5 SECONDS

**Speaker 3:**

If you've been used to giving and receiving affection, it's very hard to get used to living on your own. I can understand why people get depressed so easily if they've been used to a large family and then the day comes when there's no one there. It wasn't until I was on my own that I understood why some people turn to having a pet in the house. It keeps them company and although it can't possibly be the same, at least it means you're not absolutely alone.

PAUSE 5 SECONDS *depressing again*

**Speaker 4:**

I suppose I should be grateful for just being alive and of course I am. But I was such an active person that there are days when I find sitting at home and watching the world go by really hard. I've been used to playing sport all my life, and even my holidays would involve trying out a new sport like learning to sail or flying in a balloon. I can see all these young people kicking a ball around or whizzing past on their bikes and I'm amazed at how exhausted I feel just watching them.

PAUSE 5 SECONDS

**Speaker 5:**

Of course, in the days when I was earning a good salary, I'd think nothing of spending huge sums on eating out in expensive restaurants. I never used to worry about how much I was spending. And if I was walking past a shop and I saw something that I fancied – not that I actually needed, but just something that looked attractive like another watch or a ring – then I simply went in and bought it. Very different from today, when I have to add everything up and count my pennies to make sure I can buy even basic things like soap and toothpaste.

PAUSE 10 SECONDS

**Now you'll hear Part 3 again.**

REPEAT PART 3 – PAUSE 5 SECONDS

**That's the end of Part 3. Now turn to Part 4.**

## PART 4

**You'll hear a conversation between Isabella and Gavin, who run a small restaurant. For questions 24-30, choose the best answer A, B or C. You now have one minute to look at Part 4.**

PAUSE 60 SECONDS

**Gavin:** Have you got time to discuss what we're going to do about needing more help? *24 setting*

**Isabella:** OK. I was going to prepare the vegetables for tomorrow but I can do them later. I'm still not sure I agree with you about that, though.

**Gavin:** Look, there's simply too much for the two of us.

**Isabella:** Well, yes, when we're full, but it seems quite hard to tell when we're going to be busy. And if we have to pay someone's wages, that'll reduce our profits.

**Gavin:** But we can't carry on like this. Some days we work an eighteen-hour day! We may as well not go to bed!

**Isabella:** But if we want to open a bigger restaurant next year, then we have to watch our budget.

**Gavin:** Well, what about just opening in the evenings for dinner? That would mean we would have a little more time for ourselves.

**Isabella:** But our lunchtime trade is really good and we'd lose quite a lot of money. It's not as if business is that much better in the evenings. Our costs – you know, like the rent – would remain the same.

**Gavin:** Well then, let's put up our prices. We're one of the cheapest places in town as it is.

**Isabella:** But that's probably one of the reasons for our popularity. I mean, I know it's a tempting idea but if we're planning to expand we'll want to rely on our popularity. Why don't we think about changing our menu?

**Gavin:** What do you mean? Turn ourselves into a Chinese restaurant?

**Isabella:** Don't be silly. No, why don't we consider doing a cold buffet at lunchtimes – you know, where people can help themselves so that we're not rushed off our feet?

**Gavin:** Oh, right – and it needn't just be cold. We could have hot food as well and people could still serve themselves. We could do a range of different soups.

**Isabella:** Look, hang on. If we do all that, we'll be back where we started. We'll be spending the morning in the kitchen once again. Let's prepare salads ...

**Gavin:** It's never a good idea to make salads too far ahead.

**Isabella:** No, I know, but all the ingredients could be prepared, washed, chopped and put in the fridge overnight. It saves all that cooking for hot food.

**Gavin:** Do you think people will be disappointed if they arrive to find we've changed things?

**Isabella:** Not if we advertise it properly. We'll have new menus printed – and we'll have a fixed-price menu.

**Gavin:** Now that *is* a good idea!

PAUSE 10 SECONDS

**Now you'll hear Part 4 again.**

REPEAT PART 4 – PAUSE 5 SECONDS

**That's the end of Part 4.**

**There'll now be a pause of 5 minutes for you to copy your answers onto the separate answer sheet. Be sure to follow the numbering of all the questions.**

*[In the exam, there will be a pause of 5 minutes. You may wish to stop the recording now. Remind your students when they have one minute left.]*

**That's the end of the test. Please stop now. Your supervisor will now collect all the question papers and answer sheets.**

*miscue for 25*

# PRACTICE TEST 5

This is the Richmond First Certificate Practice Test Five. Listening. I'm going to give you the instructions for this test. I'll introduce each part of the test and give you time to look at the questions. At the start of each piece you'll hear this sound:

*Sound effect*

You'll hear each piece twice.

Remember, while you're listening, write your answers on the question paper. You'll have 5 minutes at the end of the test to copy your answers onto the separate answer sheet.

There'll now be a pause. Please ask any questions now, because you must not speak during the test.

PAUSE 5 SECONDS

Now open your question paper and look at Part 1.

## PART 1

You'll hear people talking in eight different situations. For questions 1-8, choose the best answer, A, B or C.

1   You hear a man explaining something to a child. What is he talking about?
    A   a gun
    B   a telescope
    C   a camera

PAUSE 5 SECONDS

... OK now – you see that number in the little window at the back – well, that tells you how many shots you've used. Now this button on the top – that's right, the green one – if you press that very gently, you can change the length of the lens. Now, look at these symbols on the back. There's a face – that's for shooting close-ups – and a runner – that's for taking moving images – and there's a tiny light bulb. Now, if you turn the dial to that, you can use your flash if the light is not bright enough.

PAUSE 2 SECONDS – REPEAT Q.1 – PAUSE 2 SECONDS

2   You hear a man in a market. What is he selling?
    A   watches
    B   phones
    C   jewellery

PAUSE 5 SECONDS

Come along ladies, gents, don't be shy, a once-in-a-lifetime offer! You know me – every week something different. Now you can't complain about those watches last week can you? Went in a flash, they did. And why? Value for money just like these rings. Solid silver, no joking, and look at the designs! And before you ask me where all the mobile phones are, well they sold out in less than ten minutes, so what more d'you want? Come along then, no pushing now, nice and orderly – and they all come in these lovely little boxes, all ...

PAUSE 2 SECONDS – REPEAT Q.2 – PAUSE 2 SECONDS

3   You hear two friends talking about a journey. What happened?
    A   The flight was very late.
    B   The flight was cancelled.
    C   The train was delayed.

PAUSE 5 SECONDS

**Man:**   What time did you arrive home last night?

**Woman:**   I was really late. My flight was delayed, and when we eventually landed, the last bus had left and I had to take a taxi.

**Man:**   Couldn't you have caught a train?

**Woman:**   The last train had been cancelled – I don't know why, all I know is that it was extremely expensive.

**Man:**   What a nuisance.

PAUSE 2 SECONDS – REPEAT Q.3 – PAUSE 2 SECONDS

4   You have turned on your radio. Where is the programme being broadcast from?
    A   a concert hall
    B   an open-air theatre
    C   a football stadium

PAUSE 5 SECONDS

... and as the seats fill up, there's a strong feeling of excitement in the air. Despite the warm weather, most fans are wearing their customary red and white scarves and they ... ooh, as I speak someone has just run onto the pitch – you might be able to hear the cheer from the crowd. It's only a few days since this place was packed with a very different crowd of people all shouting and stamping – just as noisily as this crowd – as they listened to the top bands ... and here they come – just listen to that roar ...

PAUSE 2 SECONDS – REPEAT Q.4 – PAUSE 2 SECONDS

5   You overhear a man talking to his colleague on the phone. What does he want to borrow?
    A   some keys
    B   a programme     *the schedule for an event*
    C   a computer

PAUSE 5 SECONDS

Well, I simply can't remember where I left my briefcase. I've rung the office and it's not on my desk. It's not in the car – it's a good job I kept my keys with me because I usually leave them in my briefcase. ... And of course I've got this meeting at 2 o'clock and the boss is expecting to check through the conference programme before next week. You couldn't possibly let me have your copy, could you? ... Oh, brilliant – thanks a lot. Could you leave it by my computer?

PAUSE 2 SECONDS – REPEAT Q.5 – PAUSE 2 SECONDS

6   You hear a girl explaining how she got a concert ticket. How did she feel at the time?
    A   amazed
    B   satisfied
    C   grateful

PAUSE 5 SECONDS

So I was standing in the queue waiting for the box office to open. There were masses of people there all hoping to get tickets at the last minute, you know, like returns which people bring back because they can't use them. People were shouting out each time a car stopped: 'I'll buy your ticket, I'll buy your ticket.' And then this huge limo drew up and a guy got out and as he walked past me he dropped his wallet, and I bent down and picked it up. I tapped him on the shoulder, handed it back and he said, 'Great, thanks' and gave me his ticket. Just like that! I couldn't believe it! 'Don't bother paying for it – just use it,' he said. And it was on the front row – one of the most expensive seats you could get. Absolutely unbelievable! And I didn't even say thank you!

PAUSE 2 SECONDS – REPEAT Q.6 – PAUSE 2 SECONDS

**7** **You hear a boy talking about a day out. Where has he been?**
   **A  an air show**
   **B  a swimming pool**
   **C  a museum**

PAUSE 5 SECONDS

Anyway, last year on my birthday we'd been to an air show, which was fantastic, and in a way I'd like to have gone again, but it seemed rather silly not to do something different. My sister suggested going to a museum, which I thought was dead boring. But this one turned out to be underwater, and you felt as if you were swimming because you're actually surrounded by all these tanks. But planes are still my favourite.

PAUSE 2 SECONDS – REPEAT Q.7 – PAUSE 2 SECONDS

**8** **You hear a woman talking to a friend. What does she want her friend to do?**
   **A  iron some clothes**
   **B  do the shopping**
   **C  cook a meal**

PAUSE 5 SECONDS

**Woman 1:** Could you do me a favour?

**Woman 2:** Of course – what is it?

**Woman 1:** Well, I've forgotten to get any milk and we've almost run out of bread. I promised Mum I'd do the ironing and she'll be home soon and she'll expect me to have a meal ready ...

**Woman 2:** Go on – so what d'you want me to do?

**Woman 1:** Well, if I rush down to the shops ...

**Woman 2:** Say no more – I've always wanted to work in a laundry!

PAUSE 2 SECONDS – REPEAT Q.8 – PAUSE 2 SECONDS

**That's the end of Part 1. Now turn to Part 2.**

## PART 2

You'll hear part of a radio programme about sleep. For questions 9-18, complete the sentences. You now have 45 seconds to look at Part 2.

PAUSE 45 SECONDS

**Announcer:** And here is Charlie Barlow to present the next item in today's programme.

**Presenter:** Did you know that we may spend up to thirty years of our lives asleep? And that ninety per cent of us say we never get enough sleep? Sleep experts reckon that we need six hours each night, but as we get older, some of us need much less sleep, perhaps only three or four hours a night.

Well, there's a club in the north of England which offers an activity four times a year. The activity is called Underground Deep Sleep. The theory is that we sleep best where it's darkest, and so the club organises an event down an old lead mine. The aim is to allow people to try out a night's sleep so deep down in the earth that there's no possibility of any light creeping in.

The idea is that a complete absence of daylight will enable people to 'sleep themselves out' and so get the amount of sleep their body requires, rather than the amount they are allowed by their alarm clock or the sun shining through the curtains.

So, would it work? Some experts are doubtful. They think that the anxiety created by the absolute blackness would prevent people from sleeping. It's also believed that you would be missing the two most important factors in a good night's rest: warmth and comfort.

However, those people who have tried the Underground Deep Sleep say that warmth is not a problem; although the mine is damp, it's not that cold. Comfort, though, is a different matter. To get into the cave, you have to crawl headfirst through a very narrow tunnel, pushing your belongings in front of you. The ceiling is very low and the floor of the cave, where people have to sleep, is rocky and uncomfortable. The roof also drips all the time, which is an added nuisance, particularly if the drips fall on your face.

But some people are very enthusiastic about the experience. They report sleeping so soundly that they can't remember their dreams. Others found the whole experience was far too much like childhood when they were so afraid of the dark that they didn't even have the courage to get up and turn on the light. But the most frightening thing for some people is thinking that the roof might collapse and fall in on top of them. In that case, people just have to shut their eyes and hope that the feeling will go away.

*Distraction?*
*in 3?*

Now, if you think you would like to take part in an Underground Deep Sleep, this is the address ...

PAUSE 10 SECONDS

**Now you'll hear Part 2 again.**

REPEAT PART 2 – PAUSE 5 SECONDS

**That's the end of Part 2. Now turn to Part 3.**

## PART 3

You'll hear five different people talking about a famous film star. For questions 19-23, choose from the list A-F which of the opinions each speaker expresses. Use the letters only once. There is one extra letter which you do not need to use. You now have 30 seconds to look at Part 3.

PAUSE 30 SECONDS

*distraction?*

**Speaker 1:**
I don't know how she does it. She's hardly ever out of the newspapers. She's either being photographed at some party or other or she's got a new boyfriend who's also famous (of course) and so she's photographed with him. I don't think I've opened a magazine or a newspaper in the last week without seeing her. She obviously doesn't mind having her photograph taken – she's not exactly what you would call camera shy, is she?

PAUSE 5 SECONDS

**Speaker 2:**
OK, the script for her last film wasn't that brilliant, but she was so wooden. There must be plenty of actresses who would have been much better in that role. I know she's very attractive and charming and she earns millions, but it must be really frustrating for some of the other actresses around who would die for a similar opportunity.

PAUSE 5 SECONDS

**Speaker 3:**
Did you see her being interviewed last night? I thought the interview was really good, very searching questions. In fact at one stage she was lost for words and seemed quite embarrassed. I suppose she doesn't like questions about how much she's worth. I noticed she avoided giving an exact figure and each time the interviewer brought up the question she managed to change the conversation. Apparently she's quite good at this technique. Makes you wonder, doesn't it?

PAUSE 5 SECONDS

**Speaker 4:**
I was listening to her agent on the radio and he was saying that he found it difficult to understand why she was so unpopular in this country. Abroad they love her. Wherever she goes, she's pursued by crowds of fans all wanting her autograph, and apparently the critics adore her as well. Very different from the critics in this country, who he thinks treat her very unfairly.

PAUSE 5 SECONDS

**Speaker 5:**
Funnily enough there was someone on my flight who knew her. He was a cameraman and had worked in the industry for years. He said that when she was on the set, she was really very nice and friendly towards everyone, and the minute she was off the set, she was incredibly rude and spoilt – like a child who always wanted its own way. He said it was like dealing with two different people. She found fault with everyone and everything and it was impossible to please her.

PAUSE 10 SECONDS

**Now you'll hear Part 3 again.**

REPEAT PART 3 – PAUSE 5 SECONDS

**That's the end of Part 3. Now turn to Part 4.**

## PART 4

You'll hear a radio discussion about an arts festival. For questions 24-30, choose the best answer A, B or C. You now have one minute to look through Part 4.

PAUSE 60 SECONDS

**Interviewer:** ... and welcome to our arts review slot. This week I have Roland Welsh with me in the studio. Roland, I believe you've just returned from a rather special weekend in Amsterdam.

**Roland:** That's right. I went to the Uitmarkt, which is held the last weekend in August. I must admit that I wasn't looking forward to it very much. I thought it looked pretty uninteresting from the information I received, but I had an absolutely fabulous time. And I've come back completely convinced that every city should have an Uitmarkt.

**Interviewer:** Well, what exactly is an Uitmarkt?

**Roland:** It marks the beginning of the new season's entertainment. The main streets and squares are filled with market stalls – not selling food but advertising the new season's performances, selling advance tickets and taking bookings. The whole atmosphere is like a fairground. But more importantly, certainly from the visitor's point of view, is that the whole weekend is given over to free entertainment. The city was absolutely packed with thousands of people who get to see and hear free music and theatre performances ...

**Interviewer:** You're joking.

**Roland:** No, I'm not, I'm not. You simply go along to whichever event you're interested in, join the queue and if it's an indoor event, then when the place is full they close the doors.

**Interviewer:** But I don't understand. How do the performers earn anything?

**Roland:** Well, they don't, I suppose. They give their services free in the hope that they'll attract an audience later in the year. It's like giving you a taste of what's to come and if you like what you see, you'll buy tickets to a proper performance.

**Interviewer:** Well, how do they fit so many different things into one weekend?

**Roland:** A lot of the events, especially the music, are held outdoors and throughout the evening. But the opera company, for example, held their performances in a concert hall. And I should also tell you that the performances only last half an hour or so. As I said, they're giving you a taste of what's to come.

**Interviewer:** But if you're a tourist, you're hardly likely to go back for a show or a concert.

**Roland:** Possibly not, but it's aimed at the Dutch first and foremost, not tourists. But I know that I personally would be prepared to go back for a weekend in order to see some of the groups. The organisation and preparation must take months. I think that's why it's so successful – because it *is* so well organised.

I know it sounds rather boring, but one of the things that struck me was how clean the streets were. I mean, that number of people and all the litter, the empty drink cans, the cartons, the paper. And during the day there were people constantly clearing away the rubbish and lorries hosing and washing down the streets. Actually, they close the main streets for most of the day, which is also another way of creating such a relaxed atmosphere because you don't have to worry about the traffic.

**Interviewer:** Would you really go all that way for an evening?

**Roland:** Well, I'd try and fit in two or three events and stay a couple of nights. And of course, because you've seen or heard what things are like, you more or less know what you're getting for your money. I think it's very clever marketing. And although it probably costs a lot to set up, it obviously works in terms of good publicity otherwise they wouldn't do it year after year.

**Interviewer:** Well, you've convinced me that it's a good idea. And as you say, it's the kind of event which could be held anywhere.

PAUSE 10 SECONDS

**Now you'll hear Part 4 again.**

REPEAT PART 4 – PAUSE 5 SECONDS

**That is the end of Part 4.**

**There'll now be a pause of 5 minutes for you to copy your answers onto the separate answer sheet. Be sure to follow the numbering of all the questions.**

*[In the exam, there will be a pause of 5 minutes. You may wish to stop the recording now. Remind your students when they have one minute left.]*

**That is the end of the test. Please stop now. Your supervisor will now collect all the question papers and answer sheets.**

# Key

## PAPER 1   Reading

| PART 1 | PART 2 | PART 3 | |
|--------|--------|--------|--------|
| 1  D | 9   C | 16 C | 24 A |
| 2  A | 10 H | 17 D ⎫ *either order* | 25 D |
| 3  C | 11 F | 18 A ⎭ | 26 B ⎫ *either order* |
| 4  C | 12 A | 19 B | 27 E ⎭ |
| 5  A | 13 E | 20 A | 28 C ⎫ |
| 6  B | 14 B | 21 D | 29 E ⎬ *any order* |
| 7  B | 15 G | 22 E | 30 B ⎭ |
| 8  D | | 23 E | |

## PAPER 2   Writing

**PART 1**

All the sample answers for the compulsory question (Part 1) have been written by students who would be expected to achieve a minimum pass grade in the FCE.

> Dear Marta,
>
> It was lovely to hear from you. I must say the travel scholarship sounds great but do you know who is offering these scholarships? You can't phone someone without really knowing who you are talking to. And there must be a form somewhere in the newspaper you got the advertisement from. The second thing which makes me suspicious is that they won't give money away to a person they've never seen before! Where are you thinking of going?
>
> I don't want to write everything negative about your idea but I'm a bit worried because it doesn't seem very safe to me. Besides, you say you are thinking of taking a year off from your job. You've only been in your new job for about three months so I think you should wait. I might even join you if you wait because I do like this idea, but I don't think we should hitchhike.
>
> I hope I didn't disappoint you too much. Give me a ring soon,
>
> Yours,
>
> Claudi

# PAPER 3   Use of English

## PART 1
1 D
2 B
3 D
4 B
5 A
6 C
7 B
8 C
9 A
10 C
11 A
12 C

## PART 2
13 of
14 order
15 its
16 any
17 on
18 away
19 who
20 their
21 night
22 like
23 to
24 According

## PART 3
25 wealthiest
26 imagination
27 construction
28 visitors
29 reality
30 lecturer
31 organisation
32 unwilling
33 appearances
34 exhibition

## PART 4

| | 1 Mark | | 1 Mark |
|---|---|---|---|
| 35 | spite of | | the heat |
| 36 | are not allowed | | to swim |
| 37 | in my | | neighbourhood |
| 38 | regret having | | missed / missing |
| OR | regret that | | I missed |
| 39 | not sweet | | enough |
| 40 | reason did Gemma | | give / have for |
| OR | was the reason | | for |
| 41 | does | | not interest |
| OR | has no interest | | for |
| 42 | is being | | brought by |

# PAPER 4   Listening

## PART 1
1 C
2 B
3 C
4 A
5 C
6 B
7 A
8 C

## PART 2
9 (she was) 12 / twelve
10 (a new) paperback / book
11 (an) engineer
12 ( a / an) (art) teacher    *either order*
13 tell her a story // read (a story) to her // read her a story
14 read her (own) stories
15 poetry / poems
16 (a new) computer
17 (an) editor
18 (the) advice

## PART 3
19 E
20 C
21 D
22 F
23 A

## PART 4
24 C
25 B
26 C
27 A
28 B
29 A
30 C

## PRACTICE TEST 2

### PAPER 1    Reading

| PART 1 | PART 2 | PART 3 | |
|---|---|---|---|
| 1  D | 9   B | 16 E | 24 E |
| 2  D | 10 H | 17 C | 25 B } either order |
| 3  A | 11 G | 18 B | 26 D |
| 4  C | 12 D | 19 E | 27 B |
| 5  B | 13 F | 20 A | 28 E |
| 6  B | 14 C | 21 A } either order | 29 A |
| 7  C | 15 E | 22 D | 30 D |
| 8  D | | 23 A | |

### PAPER 2    Writing

PART 1

---

To:      Eagle Accomodation Agency

From:   Nectaria

Sent:    April 11th

I have seen your advertisement about flats and bedsits for overseas visitors on the internet. I am going to spend six months working in England and I am trying to find somewhere to live. I would be grateful if you could send me more information and also answer some questions.

Firstly I would like to know if the flats are fully furnished and how much I can expect to pay as I don't know how much 'reasonable' means. I would also like to know if there is central heating as I shall be coming during the winter. In addition, another thing I would like to know is what 'excellent residential area' means and where your flats are. What forms of public transport are available?

Finally I would like to know about the reductions as I shall stay in London for six months and I would like a flat near the city centre for myself only.

I look forward to hearing from you as soon as possible.

Thank you.

Nectaria Loukaki

---

# PAPER 3   Use of English

**PART 1**

1  A
2  B
3  C
4  B
5  A
6  D
7  C
8  B
9  C
10  B
11  C
12  B

**PART 2**

13  the
14  than
15  its
16  for
17  part / role
18  I(i)n
19  as
20  entrance
21  despite
22  of
23  from / past
24  at / near / towards

**PART 3**

25  speciality    *specialty*
26  assignment
27  exhausting
28  equipment
29  reasonably
30  headaches
31  sleepless
32  successful
33  business
34  importance

**PART 4**

| *1 MARK* | *1 MARK* |
| --- | --- |
| 35  was prevented | from sailing by |
| 36  the most | beautiful flowers Lia |
| 37  made up | my mind to |
| 38  you know | what time it // what the time |
| 39  objects to | people interrupting |
| 40  in case | it / the weather got / was |
| 41  blamed me for | having missed / missing her / the |
| 42  had difficulty / difficulties / problems / trouble | (in) using |

# PAPER 4   Listening

**PART 1**

1  B
2  B
3  B
4  A
5  B
6  C
7  A
8  C

**PART 2**

9  porter
10  reception desk
11  (the) hotel doctor
12  24 / twenty-four hours in advance / before
13  warm clothing / clothes
14  (local) restaurants
15  until late (at night) // before / until midnight
16  credit cards
17  fined / find
18  (a) plate

**PART 3**

19  C
20  E
21  F
22  D
23  A

**PART 4**

24  C
25  C
26  B
27  B
28  A
29  B
30  C

## PRACTICE TEST 3

### PAPER 1    Reading

**PART 1**

1  D
2  B
3  C
4  C
5  D
6  A
7  D
8  B

**PART 2**

9   C
10  G
11  E
12  H
13  A
14  F
15  D

**PART 3**

16  A
17  E
18  E
19  A ⎫ *either order*
20  B ⎭
21  A
22  B
23  D

24  C
25  B ⎫ *either order*
26  D ⎭
27  E
28  B
29  E
30  C

### PAPER 2    Writing

**PART 1**

Dear Sir/Madam,

I have recently been on one of your company's exciting mystery tours by luxury coach. I am writing to explain how disappointed I was with the tour.

In the advertisement it said that the tour was in a luxury coach but instead I found the coach was dirty and old. We thought we were supposed to tour around attractive places but we only stopped once in a forest and that wasn't interesting at all. The national beauty spots and other places which you said in your advertisement didn't exist!

I was not satisfied with the unqualified guide because it was the coach driver who did all the talking. This is not all. There was no air-conditioning and we were supposed to have lunch at a famous country hotel but we went to a take-away!

Lastly when they said in the advertisement that you will not be disappointed I just laughed. I am asking for a refund because the tour was appalling. I hope to hear from you soon before I decide to take further action.

Yours faithfully,

Muizzah Mokti

## PAPER 3   Use of English

**PART 1**

1  B
2  D
3  D
4  A
5  C
6  B
7  B
8  D
9  A
10  B
11  C
12  C

**PART 2**

13  F(f)rom / S(s)ince
14  with / to
15  A(a)t
16  full
17  the
18  sailing / travelling
19  most / much
20  I(i)n
21  as
22  well
23  which / that
24  from

**PART 3**

25  worldwide
26  applicants
27  service
28  correspondence
29  opportunity
30  friendship
31  possibility / possibilities
32  relationships
33  extension
34  different

**PART 4**

|  | *1 Mark* | *1 Mark* |
|---|---|---|
| 35 | broken leg | was examined by |
| 36 | suggested | (that) we go / went // going to |
| 37 | need not / needn't<br>OR don't need | reserve<br>to reserve |
| 38 | you mind | closing |
| 39 | is not / isn't worth /<br>worthwhile | waiting |
| 40 | has given | up (drinking) |
| 41 | have not / haven't | seen Jean for |
| 42 | did not let | her / Amy stay |

## PAPER 4   Listening

**PART 1**

1  B
2  C
3  A
4  B  *A*
5  C
6  C  *B*
7  C
8  B

**PART 2**

9  2 / two / (a) couple of weeks // (a) fortnight
10  all over the world // the whole world // worldwide
11  cold / chilly / (only) 7 degrees
12  train
13  }
14  }   large / grey / very busy  – *any two*
15  learning Russian // (at a) school learning Russian
16  English (conversation) lessons
17  recipes
18  English suppers

**PART 3**

19  C
20  E
21  D
22  A
23  F

**PART 4**

24  B
25  C
26  B
27  A
28  A
29  C
30  B

## PRACTICE TEST 4

## PAPER 1    Reading

| PART 1 | PART 2 | PART 3 | |
|---|---|---|---|
| 1  A | 9   D | 16 B | 25 E⎫ either order |
| 2  D | 10 F | 17 C⎫ | 26 F⎭ |
| 3  B | 11 A | 18 D⎬ any order | 27 D |
| 4  C | 12 G | 19 F⎭ | 28 F |
| 5  C | 13 B | 20 A | 29 B⎫ either order |
| 6  D | 14 E | 21 D | 30 C⎭ |
| 7  A | 15 C | 22 E | |
| 8  B | | 23 A | |
| | | 24 C | |

## PAPER 2    Writing

## PART 1

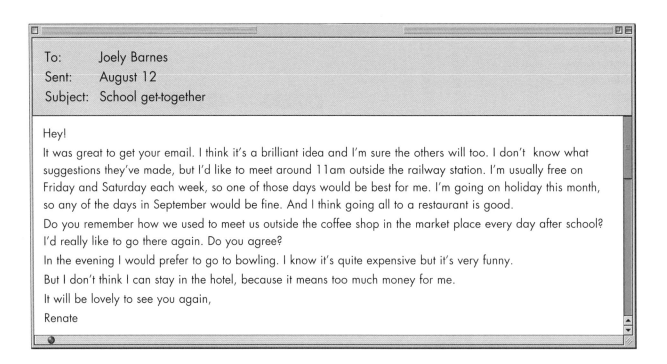

To:        Joely Barnes
Sent:      August 12
Subject:   School get-together

Hey!

It was great to get your email. I think it's a brilliant idea and I'm sure the others will too. I don't know what suggestions they've made, but I'd like to meet around 11am outside the railway station. I'm usually free on Friday and Saturday each week, so one of those days would be best for me. I'm going on holiday this month, so any of the days in September would be fine. And I think going all to a restaurant is good.

Do you remember how we used to meet us outside the coffee shop in the market place every day after school? I'd really like to go there again. Do you agree?

In the evening I would prefer to go to bowling. I know it's quite expensive but it's very funny.

But I don't think I can stay in the hotel, because it means too much money for me.

It will be lovely to see you again,

Renate

# PAPER 3   Use of English

## PART 1

1 D
2 A
3 B
4 C
5 A
6 B
7 A
8 D
9 A
10 B
11 B
12 A

## PART 2

13 not
14 few
15 the
16 B(b)ecause / A(A)s / S(s)ince
17 T(t)here
18 which / that
19 a
20 and
21 as
22 so
23 relies / depends
24 number

## PART 3

25 environmental
26 tendency
27 fifth
28 shopping
29 atmospheric
30 unattractive
31 unnecessary / needless
32 exaggeration
33 popularity
34 owners

## PART 4

| | *1 MARK* | *1 MARK* |
|---|---|---|
| 35 | will have | been married (for) |
| 36 | would not / wouldn't have | been able |
| 37 | is grown | by |
| 38 | having my car | repaired |
| 39 | wish (that) you had / you'd | got |
| 40 | and got | away with |
| 41 | had | dropped off |
| 42 | is supposed | to be / get ? |

# PAPER 4   Listening

## PART 1

1 C
2 A
3 C
4 B
5 B
6 C
7 A
8 B

## PART 2

9 Australia
10 (his) business / work // he was working    not in script
11 (a) / (the) train
12 bus / coach        *either order*
13 three quarters of an hour // 45 min(utes)
14 twenty / 20 min(utes)
15 } self-service place
16 } snack bar        *either order*
17 } chocolate
18 } shoe        *either order*

## PART 3

19 D
20 F
21 B
22 C
23 E

## PART 4

24 B
25 C
26 C
27 C
28 A
29 B
30 A

# PRACTICE TEST 5

## PAPER 1    Reading

| PART 1 | PART 2 | PART 3 | |
|---|---|---|---|
| 1  D | 9  E | 16  D | 24  A |
| 2  C | 10  F | 17  B | 25  B |
| 3  B | 11  B | 18  D | 26  C |
| 4  D | 12  G | 19  B ⎫ either order | 27  D |
| 5  B | 13  H | 20  E ⎭ | 28  A ⎫ either order |
| 6  B | 14  C | 21  A | 29  B ⎭ |
| 7  C | 15  A | 22  C ⎫ either order | 30  C |
| 8  C | | 23  E ⎭ | |

## PAPER 2    Writing

### PART 1

Dear Ms Orten,

I am the student who is going to show you around our school and our director has asked me to reply to your requests as he is very busy at present.

I am sorry that it is not possible to arrange for everything you would like, but I will explain what arrangements have been made. As you are arriving at 8.30am we will take you first to our morning assembly. Then we will show you around the classrooms and you will be able to talk to our students who are there. I will take you to the science laboratories at 11 am and there will be classes in maths, history, art and information technology to choose from if you are interested.

At 12.45pm we will have lunch in our school canteen so you can meet more students. As you are coming on Wednesday the whole school will have sport at 2pm. There won't be an orchestra on that day, unfortunately, but perhaps you would like to hear our choir.

We are looking forward to meeting you; I will meet you at the main entrance when you arrive.

Yours sincerely,

Loretta Lo

## PAPER 3    Use of English

**PART 1**

1  C
2  A
3  C
4  B
5  B
6  C
7  D
8  A
9  C
10  C
11  B
12  D

**PART 2**

13  I(i)t
14  known
15  of
16  what
17  is
18  each / every
19  A(a)nother
20  as
21  by
22  where /when
23  are
24  F(f)rom

**PART 3**

25  C(c)ompetitors
26  sporting
27  achievements
28  international
29  successful
30  determination
31  influential
32  government
33  attention
34  heights

**PART 4**

| *1 MARK* | *1 MARK* |
|---|---|
| 35  had taken | a map |
| 36  think (that) | one of the |
| 37  are employed | by |
| 38  is not | strong enough |
| 39  whose | house this |
| 40  blame me | for the car |
| 41  not know anyone | other |
| 42  despite not | having |

## PAPER 4    Listening

**PART 1**

1  C
2  C
3  A
4  C
5  B
6  A
7  C
8  A

**PART 2**

9  six / 6
10  Underground Deep Sleep
11  no light / daylight
12  warm
13  comfortable       *either order*
14  damp
15  tunnel
16  rocky
17  drips / water
18  collapse / fall (in)

**PART 3**

19  E
20  F
21  C
22  D
23  A

**PART 4**

24  A
25  B
26  B
27  C
28  A
29  C
30  C

# Mark Scheme – Writing

## Assessment

Candidates' answers are assessed with reference to two mark schemes: one based on the examiner's overall impression (the General Impression Mark Scheme), the other on the requirements of the particular task (the Task Specific Mark Scheme). The General Impression Mark Scheme summarises the content, organisation and cohesion, range of structures and vocabulary, register and format, and target reader indicated in the task. The Task Specific Mark Scheme focuses on criteria specific to each particular task.

Candidates are penalised for dealing inadequately with the requirements of the Task Specific Mark Scheme. The accuracy of language, including spelling and punctuation, is assessed on the general impression scale for all tasks.

For answers that are below length, the examiner adjusts the maximum mark and the mark given proportionately. For answers that are over-length, the examiner draws a line at the approximate place where the correct length is reached and directs close assessment to what comes before this. However, credit is given for relevant material appearing later.

The examiner's first priority is to give credit for the candidate's efforts at communication, but candidates are penalised for inclusion of content irrelevant to the task set.

## Marking

The panel of examiners is divided into small teams, each with a very experienced examiner as Team Leader. A Principal Examiner guides and monitors the marking process, beginning with a meeting of the Principal Examiner for the paper and the Team Leaders. This is held immediately after the examination and begins the process of establishing a common standard of assessment by the selection and marking of sample scripts for all the questions in Paper 2. These are chosen to demonstrate the range of responses and different levels of competence, and a Task Specific Mark Scheme is finalised for each individual task on the paper. Examiners discuss these Task Specific and General Impression Mark Schemes and refer to them regularly while they are working.

During marking, each examiner is apportioned scripts chosen on a random basis from the whole entry in order to ensure there is no concentration of good or weak scripts or of one large centre from one country in the allocation of any one examiner. A rigorous process of co-ordination and checking is carried out before, during and after the marking process.

The FCE General Impression Mark Scheme is interpreted at Council of Europe Level B2.

A summary of the General Impression Mark Scheme is given opposite. Trained examiners, who are co-ordinated prior to each examination session, work with a more detailed version, which is subject to updating.

## General Impression Mark Scheme

### BAND 5

For a Band 5 to be awarded, the candidate's writing fully achieves the desired effect on the target reader. All the content points required in the task are included* and expanded appropriately. Ideas are organised effectively, with the use of a variety of linking devices and a wide range of structure and vocabulary. The language is well developed, and any errors that do occur are minimal and perhaps due to ambitious attempts at more complex language. Register and format which is consistently appropriate to the purpose of the task and the audience is used.

### BAND 4

For a Band 4 to be awarded, the candidate's writing achieves the desired effect on the target reader. All the content points required in the task are included*. Ideas are clearly organised, with the use of suitable linking devices and a good range of structure and vocabulary. Generally, the language is accurate, and any errors that do occur are mainly due to attempts at more complex language. Register and format which is, on the whole, appropriate to the purpose of the task and the audience is used.

### BAND 3

For a Band 3 to be awarded, the candidate's writing, on the whole, achieves the desired effect on the target reader. All the content points required in the task are included*. Ideas are organised adequately, with the use of simple linking devices and an adequate range of structure and vocabulary. A number of errors may be present, but they do not impede communication. A reasonable, if not always successful, attempt is made at register and format which is appropriate to the purpose of the task and the audience.

### BAND 2

For a Band 2 to be awarded, the candidate's writing does not clearly communicate the message to the target reader. Some content points required in the task are inadequately covered or omitted, and/or there is some irrelevant material. Ideas are inadequately organised, linking devices are rarely used, and the range of structure and vocabulary is limited. Errors distract the reader and may obscure communication at times. Attempts at appropriate register and format are unsuccessful or inconsistent.

### BAND 1

For a Band 1 to be awarded, the candidate's writing has a very negative effect on the target reader. There is notable omission of content points and/or considerable irrelevance, possibly due to misinterpretation of the task. There is a lack of organisation or linking devices, and there is little evidence of language control. The range of structure and vocabulary is narrow, and frequent errors obscure communication. There is little or no awareness of appropriate register and format.

### BAND 0

For a Band zero to be awarded, there is either too little language for assessment or the candidate's writing is totally irrelevant or totally illegible.

*Candidates who do not address all the content points will be penalised for dealing inadequately with the requirements of the task. Candidates who fully satisfy the Band 3 descriptor will demonstrate an adequate performance in writing at FCE level.

*Reproduced with the permission of Cambridge ESOL*

# Mark Scheme – Speaking

## Assessment

Throughout the test candidates are assessed on their own individual performance and not in relation to each other, by two examiners. The assessor awards marks according to four analytical criteria:

- Grammar and Vocabulary
- Discourse Management
- Pronunciation
- Interactive Communication.

The interlocutor awards a mark for Global Achievement.

### Grammar and Vocabulary

This refers to the accurate and appropriate use of a range of grammatical forms and vocabulary. Performance is viewed in terms of the overall effectiveness of the language used in spoken interaction.

### Discourse Management

This refers to the candidate's ability to link utterances together to form coherent speech, without undue hesitation. The utterances should be relevant to the tasks and should be arranged logically to develop the themes or arguments required by the tasks.

### Pronunciation

This refers to the candidate's ability to produce intelligible utterances to fulfil the task requirements. This includes stress and intonation as well as individual sounds. Examiners put themselves in the position of a non-ESOL specialist and assess the overall impact of the pronunciation and the degree of effort required to understand the candidate.

### Interactive Communication

This refers to the candidate's ability to take an active part in the development of the discourse. This requires an ability to participate in the range of interactive situations in the test and to develop discussions on a range of topics by initiating and responding appropriately. This also refers to the deployment of strategies to maintain interaction at an appropriate level throughout the test so that the tasks can be fulfilled.

### Global Achievement

This refers to the candidate's overall effectiveness in dealing with the tasks in the four separate parts of the FCE Speaking test. The global mark is an independent impression mark which reflects the assessment of the candidate's performance from the interlocutor's perspective.

## Marking

Assessment is based on performance in the whole test, and is not related to performance in particular parts of the test. In many countries, Oral Examiners are assigned to teams, each of which is led by a Team Leader who may be responsible for approximately 15 Oral Examiners. Team Leaders give advice and support to Oral Examiners, as required. The Team Leaders are responsible to a Senior Team Leader, who is the professional representative of Cambridge ESOL for the Speaking tests. Senior Team Leaders are appointed by Cambridge ESOL and attend an annual co-ordination and development session in the UK. Team Leaders are appointed by the Senior Team Leader in consultation with the local administration.

After initial training of examiners, standardisation of marking is maintained by both annual examiner co-ordination sessions and by monitoring visits to centres by Team Leaders. During co-ordination sessions, examiners watch and discuss sample Speaking tests recorded on video and then conduct practice tests with volunteer candidates in order to establish a common standard of assessment. The sample tests on video are selected to demonstrate a range of nationalities and different levels of competence, and are pre-marked by a team of experienced assessors.

**Richmond Publishing**
58 St. Aldates
Oxford
OX1 1ST
U.K.

© Diana L Fried-Booth
© Richmond Publishing
Published by Richmond Publishing
Original edition published 1998
This edition published 2010

ISBN: 978-84-668-1082-1

D.L.: M-27029-2010
Printed by: Palgraphic, S.A.

The author and publishers would like to thank all the schools
and different groups of students who piloted the original
material, but we are particularly indebted to the following
schools, their teachers and individual students who gave
permission for their written work to be included:
**UK**
Ronnie Haar and Susan Firman, King's School of English,
Beckenham, Kent
Sally Garside, St Mary's Hall, Brighton, East Sussex
Wells Cathedral School, Wells, Somerset
**Greece**
Aris Mazarakis, Lamia; Chris Stavridou, Porto-Rafti; Rena
Hounda, Peania; Antoniou Karafili, Vrilisia; A Lygouri
and A Walters, Hambakis Language School, Athens; K
Paraskevopoulou, Kostea Geitona School, Vari.
**Cyprus**
M Adamidou, G C School of Careers, Nicosia
**Argentina**
Ana de Blase, Colegio San Augustín, Buenos Aires
Santa Ines School, Province of Buenos Aires

The author and publishers would like to thank *University of
Cambridge ESOL Examinations* for permission to reproduce the
sample answer sheets on pages 12-16 and the information on
pages 62-63.


**Publisher's Acknowledgements**
Cover design       Aqueduct, London / Richmond Publishing
Illustrations       Krister Flodin

**Photographs**
Thanks to the following for permission to reproduce
photographic material in this publication:
ACI AGENCIA DE FOTOGRAFÍA; GETTY IMAGES SALES
SPAIN; HIGHRES PRESS STOCK; ISTOCKPHOTO; SERIDEC
PHOTOIMAGENES CD; ARCHIVO SANTILLANA